South Central HS Library

4 7370 00010884 7

P9-DBV-445

Sayers
My Life and Times

Gale Sayers with Fred Mitchell

TRIUMPH
BOOKS

Copyright © 2007 by Gale Sayers and Fred Mitchell.

No part of this publication may be reproduced, stored in a retrieval system, or transmitted in any form by any means, electronic, mechanical, photocopying, or otherwise, without the prior written permission of the publisher, Triumph Books, 542 South Dearborn Street, Suite 750, Chicago, Illinois 60605.

Triumph Books and colophon are registered trademarks of Random House, Inc.

Library of Congress Cataloging-in-Publication Data
Sayers, Gale, 1943–
    Sayers : my life and times / Gale Sayers with Fred Mitchell.
        p. cm.
    Includes bibliographical references and index.
    ISBN-13: 978-1-57243-995-5
    ISBN-10: 1-57243-995-5
    1. Sayers, Gale, 1943– 2. Football players—United States—Biography. 3. Chicago Bears (Football team)—History. I. Mitchell, Fred. II. Title.
    GV939.S23
    [A3 2007]
    796.332092—dc22
    [B]

                                                              2007014957

This book is available in quantity at special discounts for your group or organization. For further information, contact:

Triumph Books
542 South Dearborn Street
Suite 750
Chicago, Illinois 60605
(312) 939-3330
Fax (312) 663-3557

Printed in U.S.A.
ISBN: 978-1-57243-995-5
Design by Sue Knopf
All photos courtesy of Gale Sayers unless otherwise indicated.

Dedication

I DEDICATE THIS BOOK TO ALL THE TRUE PIONEERS OF the National Football League, many of whom have gone without worldwide recognition over the years; players such as Fritz Pollard and Bobby Marshall, who were the first two African Americans to play in the NFL in the early 1920s.

I also dedicate this book to Buddy Young, a former great player whose sage advice guided a young Gale Sayers through a maze of life-changing decisions as I made the transition from college to professional football.

I offer special acknowledgment to all of the outstanding NFL players of the '50s and '60s who laid the foundation for the game today and made it possible for modern-day players to enjoy the millions of dollars that they do. Players such as Hugh McElhenny, Ollie Matson, Jim Brown, Deacon Jones, Merlin Olsen, Lenny Moore, Lem Barney, and many, many more.

I give special thanks and dedication to my mentor, George Halas, whose encouragement and wisdom made me a better football player and, more important, a better person.

And finally, I dedicate this book to my former teammate Brian Piccolo, who showed me the true meaning of life, love, and friendship.

Contents

Foreword

HAS IT REALLY BEEN 42 YEARS SINCE GALE SAYERS AND I joined the Chicago Bears as first-round draft picks?

Sometimes I wish I could tackle Father Time, but he is one tough opponent I have been unable to stop, or even slow down, for that matter. The events of Super Bowl XLI in Miami reminded me that it was indeed 1965 when Gale and I entered the National Football League. As the Bears and Indianapolis Colts squared off in that Super Bowl, it marked the first time in 21 years since Chicago appeared in the title game.

There was a lot of talk about the history of the Bears franchise during the week leading up to the Colts' 29–17 victory. And any talk about the Bears' storied history has to include Sayers and the quick and amazing impact he had on the professional game.

We had several future Hall of Fame players on our Bears teams when Gale and I played, yet we were unable to win a championship. To this day, I hear about that from fans. Why didn't we win a championship? How do you answer a question like that? Gale was the best running back in the league at the time. And we had some great players on defense. We just didn't have enough to really be successful as a team. But I wouldn't trade those years playing with him.

Gale was really something to watch. I felt I could always kid around with Gale and he was cool with it. He is just a good guy. We have always had a great relationship.

Playing defense in practice against Gale, I knew what the other teams had to go through. I had never met a guy who could stop on a dime and then go full speed in the opposite direction. I just couldn't believe this guy. He was absolutely the best.

What I admired about Gale is that he did everything. He returned kickoffs, he returned punts, and, man, could he run from scrimmage. It wasn't in vogue then to be sort of a specialist. He was a tough character. It had to be equally tough for him playing against our defense as it was for me playing against our offense in practice. But all of our efforts seemed to go for naught as far as winning a championship.

I remember meeting Gale for the first time in 1965 at an All-Star Game in Buffalo. It was just prior to the old College All-Star Game in Chicago. Then there were all of the All-America events that were held in New York that year, including the *Look* magazine session. Back in those days, you seldom saw highlight film clips of the college players the way you do today on ESPN and all the other television networks. So in New York that year I got to see a black-and-white film clip of Gale, who was known as the "Kansas Comet." I remember he was wearing high-top shoes as he returned a kickoff for a touchdown.

Then I played against him in a couple of All-Star games. Thinking back, I never faced a running back like that. He was the best. Glad we wound up being on the same team!

A lot of people do not realize how vigorously the old fledgling American Football League pursued both Gale and me in 1965. The Kansas City Chiefs also had drafted Gale that year; and the Denver Broncos selected me out of Illinois as the NFL and AFL fought for player talent.

I also remember that Gale and I were in New York in 1965 for the *Ed Sullivan Show,* and the NFL draft happened to be that Saturday. After I got back to my hotel room, there was a knock at the door. I opened the door and there was Lamar Hunt, then representing the Kansas City Chiefs. He said: "Okay, now we have to try to get Gale with us."

Playing defense in practice against Gale, I knew what the other teams had to go through. I had never met a guy who could stop on a dime and then go full speed in the opposite direction.

Well, I was pretty naïve back then. So I said: "Yeah, okay, whatever." It took me a number of years to realize what Hunt was trying to get me to do. I figured out later that he thought the deal Denver was going to offer me was going to be so out of line and extraordinary that I would be stupid to turn it down. I guess he was under the assumption that I was going to go to Denver and that would help to get Gale to the American Football League with the Kansas City Chiefs. It was kind of weird. I always remember that.

Wouldn't that have changed sports history if Gale and I had decided to play in the AFL!

My attorney at the time was Arthur Morris, and we looked at the numbers from Denver. But we had an appointment with George Halas at the Bears office, and that was the last time I ever saw or heard from anybody from Denver. And, of course, Gale turned down an offer from Kansas City.

As remarkable as Gale's Hall of Fame football career was, I am even more impressed with what he has done since he retired. I have worked hard to take advantage of some opportunities that came my way as an actor in Hollywood and on television since my playing days ended. And Gale has succeeded as a businessman, administrator, and philanthropist. His current project involving the creation of the Gale Sayers Center in Chicago to assist youngsters really intrigues me. I think it is pretty neat that Gale is opening a center for young people that will include mentoring opportunities. He has been very successful after football and he is helping a lot of people and really getting involved.

Preparing to quit is a theme Gale continually stresses to young athletes today. Success after football has a lot to do with the makeup of the person. Gale went into what he went into, and I did my thing. I thought I would always be in football, but those doors were closed to me for a while. So I had to choose other avenues. It seems like it just worked out. A lot of people say, "Oh, you were lucky," but I think you have to work to make luck.

The problem with many of today's NFL players is that with these extraordinary salaries, many guys really don't have to worry about what they are going to do afterward. But that is shortsighted. If you blow your money or someone does not represent you properly, that can have a big impact on your finances.

As remarkable as Gale's Hall of Fame football career was, I am even more impressed with what he has done since he retired.

After football, it was difficult for me to find what I liked to do second best. Football was always my first love. That certainly didn't mean that I couldn't find something else. And the proof of the pudding is where I have ended up today. I guess I could have been one of those guys who didn't prepare to quit. But things happened and through hard work I found out that, hey, there are other things besides football.

So many people who are not old enough to remember seeing Gale play for the Chicago Bears know of him through the award-winning movie *Brian's Song*. It depicts the story of the friendship between Gale and Brian Piccolo, who were the first interracial roommates in the NFL. The compelling story of their friendship still resonates nearly four decades later.

Gale and I had our numbers retired by the Bears on the same night at Soldier Field in 1994. It was a memorable event in many ways, including the fact that it was a rainy, cold Halloween night at Soldier Field. The Bears lost to the archrival Green Bay Packers that Monday night, but none of that diminished the pride I felt.

• • •

I am proud to count Gale Sayers as one of my really valued friends, and I am proud to have shared so many cherished memories with him. We will remain teammates forever.

—*Dick Butkus*

Acknowledgments

SPECIAL THANKS TO THE *CHICAGO TRIBUNE* Sports Department, in particular assistant managing editor of sports Dan McGrath, sports editor Mike Kellams, and assistant sports editor Ken Paxson; and to the Chicago Bears.

Thanks also to the staff of Triumph Books: Mitch Rogatz, Tom Bast, Mike Emmerich, and Morgan Hrejsa.

Introduction
The Game Plan

WHEN I USED TO RUN WITH THE FOOTBALL, I WAS ABLE to accomplish so much with natural instincts and God-given talent. Sportswriters often would ask me after a game: "What were you thinking when you faked out that defender and made that incredible run?"

My answer was always the same: "I wasn't thinking about anything; I just did it. It came naturally." One of my enduring quotes to NFL Films really says it all: "Just give me 18 inches of daylight. . . . That's all I need."

My football playing days were over nearly four decades ago, and I realized right away that making long runs and scoring touchdowns in life take more than gut instinct. It takes a well-conceived plan. I was aware of that even during my playing days when people called me the "Kansas Comet." I refer to that plan for life as "preparing to quit."

As I recap my childhood and many of my football accomplishments in this autobiography, I also pick up the story from the end of my playing days and focus on my subsequent life as a college sports administrator, business-man, motivational speaker, and father.

I remarried in 1973 to Ardie Agee. She is a fantastic lady, and she has a fantastic memory, which helped me piece together the many details of my life since my brief, yet memorable, days of playing for the Chicago Bears.

A big story regarding my divorce from Linda and subsequent marriage to Ardie appeared in the December 27, 1973, edition of *Jet* magazine, a Johnson publication based in Chicago that highlights the news and accomplishments of prominent African Americans. The article featured several pictures of Ardie and me in our new nine-room home in Kansas. At that time, Ardie was a nurse's assistant at Watkins Memorial Hospital, based on the University of Kansas campus where I was assistant athletics director.

My football playing days were over nearly four decades ago, and I realized right away that making long runs and scoring touchdowns in life take more than gut instinct.

Ardie and I had known each other three years by then. She was very sensitive to the rumors and gossip going around at that time because of the timing of my divorce and remarriage. Ardie told *Jet*: "I know people talk and things come up in the paper. But no one bothers to call Gale to get it from the horse's mouth, so to speak. So far, no one has said anything to me. I don't like a lot of publicity. I am active in civic things. I'm on the board of the YMCA, and I belong to some church groups."

When Ardie and I were first married, her four sons were 18, 17, 15, and 13. The oldest was in the Marines at the time, and the two middle sons attended school in Omaha, Nebraska. The youngest son lived with us in Lawrence, Kansas.

Ardie and I were into horseback riding and golf, as well as attending various sports events. In fact, our home in Kansas was bordered by a golf course. As Ardie told *Jet*: "I just want to make Gale happy." And for 35 years and counting, she certainly has.

So many people who aren't old enough to remember watching me as a football player know of me because of the movie *Brian's Song*. It is the story of my friendship with teammate Brian Piccolo after we became the National Football League's first interracial roommates in 1967.

Brian tragically passed away in 1970 from a rare form of cancer at the age of 26, but his memory endures, not only in my mind but also in the minds of the millions who have been made aware of his legacy.

Race relations in the United States have improved dramatically in many areas since the 1960s, yet we have miles to go in terms of improving awareness and tolerance. As Brian and I proved four decades ago, racial prejudice is usually fueled by ignorance and misunderstanding. By living together as roommates, each of us became more aware of the other's cultural background and traditions, and we discovered we had much more in common than we had differences. That was a great lesson for us and the rest of society.

One of the constant themes in this autobiography is my disdain for the showboat attitude displayed by many of today's pro football players. During my era, the entertainment consisted of the players performing well on the football field—running, passing, kicking, blocking, tackling. It did not include players spiking the football after scoring a touchdown, mugging in front of the camera on the sideline, or celebrating in the end zone with some contrived dance. A lot of times today, a team might be trailing by two or three touchdowns, and one of its players will perform a dance and point to the sky after sacking the opposing quarterback. What has this game come to? I blame television, in part, for drawing attention to these silly antics that take away from the integrity of the game.

I guess you could call me "old school" in terms of my appreciation for the game of football.

I am turning 64 this year as I am writing this book with the assistance of *Chicago Tribune* sports columnist Fred Mitchell. I guess you could call me "old school" in terms of my appreciation for the game of football. That's fine with me. I was only 27 when I penned my first autobiography. I am so much wiser, so much more experienced now. I hope you find these pages filled with candid opinions, refreshing honesty, and continued inspiration.

Sayers

1

Sometimes Life Brings You to Your Knees

IT WAS A PLAY WE HAD RUN DOZENS AND DOZENS OF times in 1968 with the Chicago Bears. But this time, unbeknownst to me, this play would change my football career. Ultimately, it would change the way I lived my life.

The play—"49 Toss Left"—was called in the huddle by quarterback Virgil Carter and it was designed to be run to the outside of the left tackle. It called for my blocker, Randy Jackson, to lead the way, but instead of waiting a half second for the play to unfold, I instinctively ran up on the heels of my blocker.

I planted my right leg to make a cut, but San Francisco 49ers right cornerback Kermit Alexander lunged ahead and pounced on my leg like a hungry animal.

My knee buckled as my leg remained planted awkwardly in the Wrigley Field turf. Nowhere to go, no place for it to give. I screamed in pain at the moment of impact. My football life passed before my very eyes in that instant as I gamely tried to leap to my feet. But the strength in the leg was gone, my knee wobbled. It felt numb, and for more than an instant, so did I, emotionally. I signaled to the Bears trainers along the sideline to come and get me. As my teammates carried me off the field, I passed out. And later, I was told, so did nearly thousands of Bears fans as they watched.

I had never been seriously injured on the football field and this sudden threat to my NFL career left me feeling somewhat embarrassed and definitely angry. "Why me?" I wondered. I was having my finest season in the NFL, playing in the final year of my contract.

My football life passed before my very eyes in that instant as I gamely tried to leap to my feet. But the strength in the leg was gone; my knee wobbled. It felt numb, and for more than an instant, so did I, emotionally.

Then, on the bench along the sideline, I sat alone. And I cried.

"It's gone! It's gone!" I repeated to team physician Dr. Theodore Fox. And although I wanted to hear an encouraging word, Dr. Fox soon confirmed my greatest fear. The knee had taken the full brunt of the hit, bending to about a 90-degree angle from the long axis of the thigh.

For a man who made his living with his legs—cutting and leaping, sprinting and churning—the news of losing one of those pistons was as devastating as a surgeon losing the use of one of his limbs or a pilot losing the sight in one eye.

I was carried off on a stretcher to the locker room and Dr. Fox said he would take a closer look at my knee at the hospital following the game. They wanted to operate on me right away, so they gave me some sedatives to relax me. But I was wide awake on the operating table before they finally put me to sleep.

I was so keyed up I kept asking the medical personnel about the score of the Bears game. I finally learned that we had beaten the 49ers 27–19. But my toughest personal challenge lay ahead in the many months of rehabilitation.

I remember Dr. Fox promising me that he would make my severed knee "as good as, if not better than, it was before." I was on the operating table for three hours and I would later learn that the ligaments on the medial side were destroyed, as well as the anterior cruciate ligament.

After coming out of the operating room, I realized I was in the intensive care facility and I had a 15-pound cast on my right leg from my hip to my toes. Dr. Fox was there when I came to and the anesthetic began to wear off. He assured me the operation was a success, and, sure enough, I was walking on crutches two days later. The following day—a Wednesday—I didn't want anything to do with the crutches. So I began walking on one leg. By the end of the week we held a press conference at the hospital as I was discharged.

It had been an emotional day for me, an emotional week. Dr. Fox and I spoke privately before I left the hospital. I thanked him for all he had done, and I became choked up as tears filled my eyes. But I knew this would be the last time I could afford to feel sorry for myself.

I remember taking 500 telegrams and about 75 letters home with me from the hospital from friends and fans wishing me a speedy recovery. That meant a lot to me.

I would say that most of the letters were from kids. One letter came from a young boy who lived in the South, right after the 1968 presidential election. The letter read: "I was sorry to see you get hurt, Mr. Sayers. I was talking to my father. He heard that George Wallace, when he became president, was going to send all the Negroes back to Africa. I didn't want George Wallace to become president because I didn't want to see you go back to Africa."

The injury was a crippling blow that later would serve as a painful metaphor for the rest of my life. I have continued to overcome obstacles in my postfootball career to become successful as a college administrator, businessman, and parent. I became determined—no, *obsessed*— to come back from this horrible physical mishap. I would get up and show the world that I could not be stopped by one vicious blow. I would return, stronger than ever, better than ever. And I would never leave myself in such a vulnerable situation in my life. I would continue to prepare to play professional football to the very best of my ability. And at the same time I would prepare to lead the rest of my life with confidence, grit, and purpose, even when life seemed to cut me down at the knees.

I never held any personal resentment or bad feelings toward Alexander. I have seen and spoken with him in subsequent years. It was a clean hit and it was just unfortunate that I was in the wrong place at the wrong time in terms of my body's position.

Alexander was a fine athlete who played for the Los Angeles Rams and Philadelphia Eagles, as well as the 49ers. In 1968, the year Alexander's tackle ended my season, he would wind up the year with nine interceptions, including one that he returned 68 yards for a touchdown. He also recovered four fumbles. At 5′11″, 185 pounds, Alexander also was an accomplished punt and kickoff return man.

In 1984, Alexander had something infinitely more tragic than a busted knee happen in his life. According to a United Press International article, his mother, Ebora Alexander, his sister, Dietra Alexander, and two of his nephews were brutally murdered within their own middle-income South Los Angeles home. The two suspects implicated in the slaying would later be caught and identified. I cannot begin to imagine enduring such a devastating loss.

I became determined— no, obsessed— to come back from this horrible physical mishap. I would get up and show the world that I could not be stopped by one vicious blow.

Back in December 1968, Dr. Fox removed the burdensome cast that had been rubbing up against the incision for four weeks. He replaced the hard cast with a more manageable five-pound cast. It made me feel much more mobile and I wanted to bend my knee, but I couldn't. It was the weirdest feeling. Dr. Fox had warned me that I would not be able to bend it immediately. Because of all the adhesions, it took me about two weeks before I finally could straighten it out and then bend it again.

I began the arduous process of rehabbing my knee through physical therapy. I enrolled in a gym class at the Lawson YMCA in Chicago, where a former NFL player,

Dick Woit, put me through the most rigorous workouts I could ever imagine. His theory was: "Physical condition is your recuperation power after you've had physical exertion." Workouts six days a week included sit-ups, leg lifts, weight lifting, push-ups, and running up and down the fire escape to the parking lot in the back of the building. And, amazingly, Woit performed all of the drills that we did in the class.

He repeatedly told me that the operation was a success but that I needed to be vigilant about conditioning the knee to ensure its full recovery.

I would continually check in with Dr. Fox to get updates on the condition of my knee. He repeatedly told me that the operation was a success but that I needed to be vigilant about conditioning the knee to ensure its full recovery.

I gradually increased my distance on my jogging routes, going three or four miles at a time near a park where I lived. Jesse Jackson lived near me in those days and we would often toss the football around in the park. He was quite an athlete in high school and college, a quarterback, in fact. So we spent a lot of time together and became good friends.

I was filled with regret when I had to miss the last five games of the 1968 season. I felt I had been headed for the best season of my life and we had a great chance to win our division. In fact, we could have if we had won the last game of that season. But Green Bay won, 28–27.

My cast was later auctioned off for a good cause. A high school football player, Gary Steger of Lake Park High School in Roselle, Illinois, had been paralyzed in a game. A foundation had been started for him and George Gillett, then president of the Harlem Globetrotters, purchased it for $3,500 to benefit Steger's foundation.

I recently learned through an online Lake Park High School alumni release that the 11th annual Gary Steger Golf Outing was held June 16, 2006, at the Schaumburg Golf Club. The golf outing benefits a memorial scholarship given in Gary's name to graduating seniors from Lake Park High School and other Lake Park Educational Foundation projects, and the Marklund Home, which serves students with disabilities.

Steger was a star on the Lancer football team in 1968 before he was injured playing football and became a quadriplegic. The golf outing originally helped fund living expenses for Gary in his long-term care. When Gary passed away on May 19, 2002, the family and organizers of the golf event decided to keep the event going in his name and fund scholarships and other charities. I think that is a terrific gesture.

• • •

I used to love playing football in Wrigley Field, which is better known today as the historic home of the Chicago Cubs. The NFL made the Bears move out of Wrigley Field because it did not hold the minimum of 50,000 fans. That was a shame because we felt we had a real home-field advantage there. Of course, if we were not playing particularly well as a team, the fans were right on top of us at Wrigley Field and we would hear the boos and catcalls from the crowd, almost as if they were standing right next to us. I remember seeing the empty beer cups being tossed our way as we headed to the locker room following a loss. But I also remember being able to slap hands and give high-fives to the smiling fans on the way to the locker room following a victory.

I used to love playing football in Wrigley Field...

One of the neat things about Wrigley Field was the fact that bleachers were added to increase capacity and put more fans closer to the action. Eventually the Bears organization acquired a large, portable bleacher section that spanned the right- and center-field areas. This East Stand raised Wrigley's football capacity to about 46,000. After the Bears left, those East bleachers were transported to Soldier Field as the North Stand, until they were replaced by permanent seating.

When I think of Coach Halas, I also think about the way he helped us focus and concentrate on the home games at Wrigley Field. The conditions weren't always the best there. For instance, we dressed in the old locker room that the Chicago Cubs used, which would have been in the left-field corner of Wrigley. Believe me, those were some tight quarters, especially when you consider that an entire 45-man football team, coaching staff, and trainers were crammed in there. I think there were four or five showers in that whole locker room for the entire team. And half the time the water was cold. Still, that was our home stadium and we tried to make sure we enjoyed a home-field advantage when we played there.

Like many NFL fields that were shared with baseball teams back then, the sod that covered the infield would become undone during games, especially when it was cold. There were no dome stadiums or AstroTurf fields back then, but Coach Halas made sure we appreciated the fact that we were able to play professional football in front of the most passionate fans in all of sports.

Young people today who attend Cubs baseball games probably wonder how in the world the Bears could have fit a football field inside Wrigley Field. Believe me, it wasn't easy. The football field ran north to south—from left field to the foul side of first base. The remodeling of the bleachers made it an even tighter fit. As a matter of fact, the corner of the south end zone was in the visiting baseball team's dugout, which was filled with pads for safety. That required a special ground rule that sliced off that corner of the end zone. One corner of the north end line ran just inches short of the left-field wall.

Of course, if we were not playing particularly well as a team, the fans were right on top of us at Wrigley Field and we would hear the boos and catcalls from the crowd, almost as if they were standing right next to us.

There is a legend described in the Pro Football Hall of Fame archives that Bronko Nagurski, the Hall of Fame Bears fullback, once bulldozed his way through the defense and then ran all the way through that end zone before slamming his head on the bricks. And they wore leather helmets back then!

Nagurski supposedly went back to the bench and told Coach Halas, "That last guy gave me quite a lick!" That incident must have been why the Bears decided to put some padding in front of that wall.

But Wrigley Field retains some cherished memories for many longtime Bears fans. The Bears are second only to the Green Bay Packers in total NFL championships, and all but one of those came during their tenure at Wrigley. The Bears called Soldier Field home the year they captured Super Bowl XX. After a half-century at Wrigley Field, the NFL instituted its rule of requiring each stadium to seat at least 50,000 fans. I remember that the Bears had one experimental game at Dyche Stadium on the Northwestern University campus, but otherwise continued at Wrigley until the team transferred to Soldier Field on the lakefront.

It was difficult for me to watch the film of me injuring my knee at Wrigley Field. One night, my first wife, Linda, and I had some friends over to the house. Two of my teammates—George Seals and Frank Cornish—were among the guests. I pulled out the projector after dinner so we could watch the Bears' 1968 highlight film.

When the film sequence that showed my injury came on, Seals tried to be funny. "Get up! Get up!" Seals shouted. I did not find it amusing and I got a strange feeling throughout my body, just recalling and reliving the devastation of that moment. After the guests left, I told Linda that I would never again look at that film.

• • •

I felt invigorated going into the 1969 season. I had signed a new three-year contract that made me the highest-paid player in the NFL, I was in great physical condition, and I had been named the first-string running back on the All-Time Pro Football Team in conjunction with the 50th anniversary of the league. I felt that was quite an honor, especially since I had played in just three-and-a-half pro seasons. I had been picked over such greats as Red Grange, Hugh McElhenny, and George McAfee.

I managed to return to the Bears' lineup in 1969 and run for 1,032 yards in a 14-game season, winning a second rushing title. When I was presented with the George Halas Award as "the most courageous player in professional football," I dedicated the prize to my friend, roommate, and teammate, Brian Piccolo, who was dying of cancer.

I decided to retire because of my loss of speed. My final game was in the preseason. I had three carries and fumbled twice. By halftime, I told coach Abe Gibron I was going to retire.

In 1970, I suffered a second knee injury, this time to my left knee. After another rehabilitation period, I tried for a comeback but was not successful. I decided to retire because of my loss of speed. My final game was in the preseason. I had three carries and fumbled twice. By halftime, I told coach Abe Gibron I was going to retire. And after that game Gibron told the rest of the team of my plans. That was it.

After that, I began multiple endeavors, including a career as CEO of a computer company in 1983. In 1977, I was inducted into the Pro Football Hall of Fame. And in 1994, I had my uniform, No. 40, retired at Soldier Field in Chicago. On the same evening, my contemporary and friend Dick Butkus was similarly honored with the retiring of his No. 51. I have discovered that life after football can also be very rewarding. Just as in sports, you get out of life what you put into it. In 1973 I returned to

While some former sports figures fade away into obscurity after their glory years, I want to continue to grow and prosper while helping others.

Kansas to work as an assistant athletics director. And I soon became associated with the Williams Educational Fund, the primary fund-raising body for the Kansas Athletics. During that period I found time to earn my master's degree in educational administration.

After four years at Kansas, I went back to take the athletics director position at Southern Illinois in 1976. After five years in that position, I returned to Chicago and formed my own sports marketing and public relations firm, which evolved into Sayers Computer Source. The firm began in 1982 as a computer supplies reseller. Since the company's founding, Sayers Computer Source has grown to include four branches across the United States with revenues of more than $150 million. The firm also has expanded its services to more than just selling computers. We also offer operating systems, systems integration, and consulting services.

In 1999 I was inducted into the Chicago Area Entrepreneurship Hall of Fame, my first nonsports Hall of Fame. And what an honor that was for me.

Then that summer Ernst & Young named me as one of the Technology/Communications Entrepreneurs of the Year. Upon accepting the award I said, "This is more significant than my induction into the National Football League Hall of Fame because the latter was the result of God-given talents and the former is the result of my hard work and recognition of personal achievements."

I was proud to donate $75,000 as a gift to my alma mater in 1999, to be used to establish the Gale Sayers Microcomputer Center in the School of Education. While some former sports figures fade away into obscurity after their glory years, I want to continue to grow and prosper while helping others.

2

Papa Bear and Me

ALTHOUGH GEORGE HALAS HAD THE UNFLATTERING reputation of being cheap with many other players, I found him to be particularly generous in my situation. Each of my first four seasons on the Bears, he gave me a sizeable incentive bonus at the end of the year.

I recall meeting Mr. Halas for the first time. Being a quiet and shy first-round draft pick out of Kansas in 1965, I was rather intimidated meeting him. But I was brought up to respect older people, and I never had a problem with Coach Halas. All he wanted you to do was to show up in shape and give 100 percent. And I did that. A lot of players wouldn't come to training camp in shape. And three weeks into camp, we had our first exhibition game. You can't get in shape in three weeks.

I have said so many times that I love George Halas and that we had a father-son relationship. He was someone I could always come and talk to about almost anything. After the misunderstanding I had with Otto Graham when he thought I was dogging it during practice for the College All-Star Game in 1965, Coach Halas said he would judge me solely on what I did in training camp with the Bears.

I didn't have an agent when I negotiated a contract my rookie year. Buddy Young, who worked for the NFL at the time, was my mentor and he helped me in my negotiations. It's true Coach Halas was tight-fisted with a dollar, but my contract back then was in line with the contracts of other running backs who were coming into the league.

"If Gale Sayers can run all the way to the goal line, we all can run to the goal line." So for the next 20 minutes or so, everyone had to run hard in practice, all the way to the goal line. Some of the players were pissed off at me..."

When it came to practice, I always came to play. I ran full speed every play and a lot of players didn't do that. But I knew that was what I had to do to be in shape.

I remember one Bears practice in particular from my rookie year. The ball was on the 50-yard line and I took the hand-off and ran all the way to the goal line. Coach Halas stopped practice when he saw me do that. He said: "If Gale Sayers can run all the way to the goal line, we all can run to the goal line." So for the next 20 minutes or so, everyone had to run hard in practice, all the way to the goal line. Some of the players were pissed off at me, but I'm sorry, that's me. That's the way I had to get in shape because I knew I was going to be keyed on during the games. That's the way I did it in college at Kansas. That was the only way I knew. Coach Halas appreciated it, but a lot of the veterans didn't.

When I first came to the Bears, Coach Halas was 70 years old. I couldn't believe it. I don't know how he survived those cold Chicago winters we had in the 1960s. He was the first man on the field and the last one to leave the field. He was just a great individual. That inspired me, just seeing him on the field. If he could stay out there at age 70 and I was just 21 years old, I knew I had to do it.

Chicago fans also loved George Halas and respected all that he did for that franchise. Don't get me wrong, the fans booed when we didn't play well, including that disastrous 1969 season when we went 1–13. But the main thing they asked from us was a solid and all-out effort. That was one thing we all could control.

I tied an NFL record by scoring six touchdowns during one muddy game against the San Francisco 49ers at Wrigley Field in 1965. My six touchdowns included an 80-yard pass reception, a 50-yard rush, and an 85-yard punt return. But Halas didn't say anything special to me after that performance.

Back then, we weren't interested in records or anything like that. If you got ahead by 20 points, you took out the first string and put in the second string. I probably could have scored eight touchdowns that particular day. It didn't make any difference, and we wanted to win the ballgame. After that game, Halas just said: "You had a great game." And that was it. That's all I wanted to hear. We went about our business and things worked out.

I respected Halas as a coach and as a man. Of course, as I mentioned earlier, he could be a tough negotiator. Halas had a disdain for player agents and attorneys, so we always had to represent ourselves in negotiations for new contracts. When I went in to talk to him about a new contract, I remember the conversation went something like this:

"Have you thought about what you want, Gale?"

"Yes."

"What do you think you'd like to receive?"

"I want $500,000 for three years," I blurted out.

Halas grumbled and said, "Impossible. There's no way I can do this. It's not feasible for me to give you so much money."

I said, "Okay, I'll talk to you later."

I went back to Halas three days later and said, "Coach, I don't want to play games with you and I know you don't want to play games with me. But I do think I'm worth $100,000 a year."

In our next meeting, we were pretty close to getting things settled when Halas's late son, George Halas Jr., entered the room. He was known as Muggs, and he was not eager to pay me that kind of money.

Muggs said, "Consider yourself lucky. If my father didn't like you as much as he does, you wouldn't be getting that much."

With that comment, I got up and walked out of the room. I didn't talk to Coach Halas about the contract for another two weeks. Muggs was not there the next time and Coach Halas said, "Gale, let's settle it now." So I signed the three-year contract that I wanted.

Another memory about Coach Halas that sticks out in my mind involves his response to the tragic death of

Brian Piccolo. I remember that the team was very, very somber after he lost his battle with cancer in 1970. The team took it badly, and I know that Coach Halas took it badly as well. In addition to the shock of his loss, it turned out that the final hospital bill for Brian was over $500,000. And Halas took care of all of it. He also made sure that all three of Brian's daughters were able to go to college. That was the kind of man he was.

To this day, it still amazes me how Halas basically parlayed a dream into establishing the Bears as a franchise and helped lay the groundwork for the National Football League. I guess it all started with the Staley Starch Works of Decatur, Illinois. According to the Pro Football Hall of Fame, it was that company's president, A.E. Staley, who encouraged Halas onto the pro football scene in 1920. Then Halas helped get the entire league started.

Back then, we weren't interested in records or anything like that. If you got ahead by 20 points, you took out the first string and put in the second string.

His contributions to the game as a player, as a coach, and as a club owner and executive seem inconceivable today.

I always judge a man by the way he treats me. I learned in later years that Halas did not have the best reputation when it came to black players. In fact, historians have said Halas played an integral part in the segregation of the league in the 1930s by refusing to sign black players to the Bears. Fritz Pollard, who in the 1920s was the league's first African American coach, blamed Halas for keeping him out of the league later on, in the 1930s and 1940s.

Pollard was born in Chicago and starred at Lane Tech High School. In college Pollard led Brown University to the 1915 Rose Bowl as an All-American running back. His team beat strong opponents such as Yale and Harvard.

Muggs said, "Consider yourself lucky. If my father didn't like you as much as he does, you wouldn't be getting that much."

During a *New York Times* interview in 1978, Pollard recalled the hatred he faced as a player. "They had some prejudiced people there. I had to get dressed for games in [team owner] Frank Neid's cigar factory. The fans booed me and called me all kinds of names. You couldn't eat in the restaurants or stay in the hotels."

The NFL did not have black players from 1934 to 1946. In 1964, Arthur Daley of *The New York Times* wrote, "Can the [Hall of Fame] committee continue to skip past such vaunted pioneers from the first-team periods as Paddy Driscoll, Benny Friedman, Joe Guyon, Keith Molesworth, and Fritz Pollard, to name only a few?"

In 1978, columnist Jerry Izenberg wrote of Pollard, "It is a shame and a scandal that more young people do not even know his name. Those numbers add up to nothing in Canton, Ohio. He is not a member of the Pro Football Hall of Fame. That is an incredible oversight—almost as incredible as the chain of events which form Pollard's own personal history."

Pollard's daughter Leslie told the *Boston Globe*'s Joe Burris, "It's strange. This generation doesn't know anything. Almost all of my younger life, there was mention of my father in his football days almost every time you picked up a newspaper. Now, people have never heard of him."

I was pleased to see that the Senior Selection Committee for the Pro Football Hall of Fame made a historic decision by picking Pollard as one of two senior nominees for the Class of 2005.

Halas eventually saw the light to help to integrate the league. He drafted the NFL's first black player since 1933, George Taliaferro, although Taliaferro did not play for the Bears; Halas later signed Willie Thrower out of Michigan State. Thrower became the league's first black quarterback with the Bears, although he lasted just one year.

Halas had a disdain for player agents and attorneys, so we always had to represent ourselves in negotiations for new contracts.

Halas was an NFL pioneer in other ways. He made the Bears the first team to hold daily practice sessions, to analyze film of opponents, to place assistant coaches in the press box during games, and to broadcast games by radio. He also offered to share the Bears' television revenue with teams in smaller cities. He knew that would be best for the league in the long haul.

Halas was a charter member of the Pro Football Hall of Fame in 1963. In fact, the Hall of Fame is located on George Halas Drive in Canton, Ohio. Also, the NFC championship trophy bears his name. To this day, the jerseys of the Chicago Bears have the initials "GSH" on their left sleeves in tribute to George Stanley Halas, and I still wear my feelings on my sleeve for Coach Halas.

In 1993, Miami Dolphins coach Don Shula finally surpassed Halas's victory total of 324. Shula coached the Baltimore Colts from 1963 to 1969 and the Miami Dolphins from 1970 to 1995. In 1995, he concluded his 33rd season as the winningest NFL head coach ever with a career mark of 347–173–6 (.665). Shula's team reached the playoffs 20 times in 33 years and his teams won at least 10 games 21 times.

Of all the NFL coaches, only Shula and Halas attained 300 victories.

3

Remembering Brian

AS YOU MIGHT EXPECT, SO MUCH HAS HAPPENED IN MY life since the original television movie, *Brian's Song*, was made back in 1971.

Frankly, I was surprised by the enormous reaction to the movie that won five Emmys. Perhaps that is because I actually lived the experience. That film was made during a time when race riots and blatant acts of discrimination were occurring across the nation. So many people who have seen the movie know about me simply from *Brian's Song* and not as a former professional football player. People will stop me at the airport or on the street and say, "Hey, I loved that movie about you and Brian Piccolo; it really brought me to tears."

The movie was made in Hollywood while I was in training camp with the Bears in Rensselaer, Indiana. Believe me, if you have ever been to Rensselaer, you know it is nothing like Hollywood. There is no glitz or glamour there, and that is exactly the way Coach Halas wanted it for his Bears players during summer training camp.

Even though I was at camp, I was able to consult somewhat on the movie. Billy Dee Williams, a very popular and handsome young actor at the time, played me in the movie. I was flattered that the movie directors would choose Billy Dee Williams, but I must admit that I had some reservations at first because he was very slightly built and he did not look all that athletic to me. I would have preferred to play my role myself, but the fact that the movie was filmed during training camp made it impossible for me to pull that off. So I got over that concern pretty quickly and Billy Dee certainly did a fine job in the movie.

I would have preferred to play my role myself, but the fact that the movie was filmed during training camp made it impossible for me to pull that off.

Most people don't know that Bernie Casey, who played the part of my former teammate, J.C. Caroline, actually wanted to play my part in the movie. But the directors decided he was too tall at 6′4″ to resemble me, so they stuck with their decision to have Billy Dee play my part.

Bernie was a terrific receiver during his NFL playing career for the 49ers and Rams in the 1960s. And his many talents extend beyond football. He has been a well-respected movie actor, painter, poet, and movie director for many years.

Joy Piccolo and I spent about a month together with James Caan and Billy Dee, discussing Brian's peculiar mannerisms. We talked about everything from the way Brian laughed when he told a joke to the way he handled the pain and agony of having to endure that horrible disease. Caan played the role of Brian in the movie with tremendous passion and skill.

Just as in any movie, there were a few embellishments in this one to make it more appealing. But for the most part they stuck to what really happened during my all-too-brief friendship with Brian. For example, in the scene in which I received the Most Courageous Player award and dedicated it to Brian, the movie directors had Billy Dee Williams stuttering and stammering throughout the speech. In fact, I had improved my speech pattern a great deal at that point of my life and career and delivered a smoother rendition than what you heard.

"I love Brian Piccolo, and I'd like all of you to love him," I said that night. "And when you hit your knees to pray tonight, please ask God to love him, too." I accepted the award in Piccolo's name, saying, "Compare his courage with what I am supposed to possess." I taped Brian's name over my own on the trophy.

Also, it was said that James Caan had to slow down in some running scenes so it would appear that Billy Dee was the faster halfback.

I was obviously pleasantly surprised at the enormous reaction from people about that movie. I have had people come up to me and say, "You know what, Gale? After watching that movie, we decided to name our baby after you."

Jack Warden played the role of George Halas, Shelley Fabares was Joy Piccolo and Judy Pace played the part of Linda, my wife at the time. All the actors did a wonderful job, including Bernie Casey. David Huddleston played the part of Ed McCaskey, who was Halas's son-in-law and one of the people who suggested that Brian and I become the league's first interracial roommates. Several former Bears players and coaches played themselves in the movie, including Ed O'Bradovich, Jack Concannon, and Abe Gibron.

Not a day goes by that I don't think about Brian.

Brian's Song actually was a made-for-TV movie. The story was such a success on television, however, that it was later shown in theaters. A remake was filmed in 2001 for ABC's *The Wonderful World of Disney*, starring Mekhi Phifer and Sean Maher. The film was written by veteran screenwriter William Blinn.

Even the musical theme to the original *Brian's Song*, "The Hands of Time," became a popular tune during the early 1970s.

I was obviously pleasantly surprised at the enormous reaction from people about that movie. I have had people come up to me and say, "You know what, Gale? After watching that movie, we decided to name our baby after you." That is quite flattering, of course. Sometimes I don't know just what to say to them in response to that. But the movie really did seem to hit people that way. Many people have that movie on DVD now. I seem to get more comments from white people than black people who saw the movie. I think probably more white people had TVs back in the '70s, although I don't know if that would be why exactly. I have never figured that out.

• • •

Not a day goes by that I don't think about Brian. Even when I traveled to Miami in January 2007 for Super Bowl Week in advance of the Bears playing the Indianapolis Colts, I was reminded of Brian's upbringing in Florida.

"He had a cancer that was vicious and we were so young and had no clue," his wife, Joy, said during an interview with CBS television in Chicago. "I think we believed he was going to make it, but he didn't have a prayer and now that cancer is 50 percent curable." Indeed, embryonal-cell carcinoma has a much higher cure rate today because of medical advances. Joy has since remarried and is now Joy Piccolo O'Connell.

Virginia McCaskey, George Halas's daughter, conducted an interview with the Chicago media after the Bears won the NFC championship game against the New Orleans Saints in January 2007. She spoke of the many changes in the operation of the ballclub.

"In the early years, there wasn't any money to do anything. Things that my dad did to help people were always private," she said. "One of the biggest changes to the present day goes back to the Brian Piccolo situation that brought about cancer research at Sloan-Kettering and the wonderful cure rate now of the cancer that killed Brian Piccolo. Now we're more involved in other kinds of cancer research. You can't do everything. This is [funded] mainly through the Bears Care gala."

Brian, or "Pick," as everyone called him, started rooming with me in 1967. At the time, I tried not to make a big deal out of the fact he was white and I am black. Big deal. But growing up where I did, and growing up where Brian did . . . naturally there were going to be some things that would come up that tested our comfort zones.

Brian, or "Pick," as everyone called him, started rooming with me in 1967. At the time, I tried not to make a big deal out of the fact he was white and I am black. Big deal. But growing up where I did, and growing up where Brian did ...naturally there were going to be some things that would come up that tested our comfort zones.

Pick told me that he had never really known a black person and he said strange things such as, "Are they really different? Do they sleep in chandeliers, or what?" Silly things like that. But even though we may have been naïve about each other's backgrounds, we were never afraid to ask questions. And we certainly kidded each other enough that it didn't matter if you had black skin or white skin. You simply had to have thick skin.

One time a writer came in our room to interview us about being interracial roommates.

"What do you fellas talk about?" the writer asked.

"Mostly race relations," I answered.

Then Pick chimed in, "Nothing but the normal racist stuff."

Then the writer asked, "If you had your choice, who would you want as your roommate?"

I looked him in the eye and said, "If you're asking me what white Italian fullback from Wake Forest, I'd say Pick."

Brian and I started rooming together in Birmingham, Alabama, of all places, for an exhibition game. That was a city of tremendous racial unrest in the 1960s. I was already in the room when Pick came in.

"What are you doing here?" he said.

"We're in together," I answered.

He looked a little shocked and surprised, but I had already been apprised of the situation by Bears officials. I had been asked if I minded rooming with Brian. I said that I had no problem with that. I had been rooming before with a player who had been cut. Brian had been rooming with quarterback Larry Rakestraw. The Bears decided they should pair up players who played the same position. And I think it was one of our veteran cocaptains, Bennie McRae, who suggested we should start some integrated rooming. So Pick and I were the first to try it.

Knowing the tense social climate in Birmingham at that time, Brian and I didn't have dinner together that weekend. We joked about that as we went our separate ways. In fact, that first year we probably had dinner together just two or three times.

Otherwise, I would go out with the guys I previously hung out with and Pick would socialize with his buddies on the team. Looking back now, I may have been a little distant at first, especially on game day. Pick knew to leave me alone on game day because I was in my own little moody world then.

As time went on, our personalities sort of balanced each other out. He was an extrovert and always telling jokes. I was quieter and shy the first couple of years with the Bears. One time he read a letter to me that he received from a bigoted man. It said: "I read where you stay together with Sayers. I am a white man! Most people I know don't want anything to do with them. I just don't understand you. Most Italians I have met say they stink—and they really do."

Pick told me that he had never really known a black person and he said strange things such as, "Are they really different?"

And the guy signed his name.

Social and racial progress was coming around slowly in America during that era. There was the *Brown* decision in 1954, the Civil Rights Act of 1964, and the Voting Rights Act in 1965.

Since that time African Americans have experienced more opportunities in all fields of endeavor. I can't help but believe that the black struggle for civil rights also inspired other rights movements for Native Americans, Latinos, and women.

My relationship with Brian was just a snapshot of what could be accomplished if people of different ethnic backgrounds took the time to get to truly know one another.

One game in 1967, Pick got the game ball following a contest against Minnesota. It seemed as if when I had a good game, Brian would play well also. And of course in the game that I tore up my knee against San Francisco in 1968, Brian came in and rushed for 87 yards on 18 carries. He also caught four passes for 54 yards. Against New Orleans that year, he rushed for 112 yards.

Piccolo was born in Massachusetts but raised in Fort Lauderdale, Florida. He was the big man on campus at Wake Forest as an All-American halfback. As a senior, he led the nation in scoring and rushing. Still, he wasn't drafted. The so-called NFL experts questioned his size and speed. But they couldn't measure his heart. The Bears signed him as a free agent, making it a real long shot for him to make the roster.

But each year Brian did enough to make the squad. He would say, "If I am told to do something, I do it. If I am told to block the linebacker, I do it. I am a ballplayer's ballplayer. They have got to go with me."

The first time I met Brian was at the All-American Game in Buffalo, New York, following my senior year at Kansas. In fact, four future Bears were in that game: Dick Butkus, Jimmy Jones, Pick, and me. I was very shy then and didn't say much to anybody. A lot of people, including Pick, took my shyness for arrogance. Pick said that I must have thought of myself as "a real hotshot" then.

Butkus was pretty much the same way then. He didn't have much to say to the other players either. He let his actions on the football field speak for him.

Everyone made such a big deal out of the fact that Brian and I were the NFL's first interracial roommates. Instead of trying to discover our differences, we mainly realized how much we had in common. But we did joke a lot to lighten any tension. I was No. 40 and Brian was No. 41 with the Bears, and our lockers were right next to each other. Dick Gordon, who is black, had a locker nearby. So Brian used to say, "I feel like an Oreo cookie."

Brian was my backup, and Coach Halas never liked to take me out of the game unless I was injured. So Brian had to be ready to come in the game when I got exhausted and took myself out. Sometimes Brian would have to coordinate with the running backs coach, Ed Cody, to make sure he could come in and take over for me when I got tired. Then Cody might have to go to Coach Halas to get the final okay. Fortunately, I didn't have to leave the game because of exhaustion too often. At one point, the coaches finally left it up to me and Brian to work out a system for when he should take over for me.

Besides me, I think Ralph Kurek was Brian's next closest friend on the team. Ralph had played fullback at Wisconsin before joining the Bears and he and Brian used to run around a lot together as Bears teammates.

Brian was so likeable and easy to get along with that all of the Bears players took a liking to him. After he got sick with cancer and had to be hospitalized, as soon as the team left the practice field we would all go to the hospital to see Brian. He could joke about his sickness. When we went into his room, he was never down or anything, even though the doctors had to have told him that he was in very serious danger.

Coach Halas and all of us on the team thought the doctors had gotten all of the cancer after Brian's first operation. But then he kept having this cough that wouldn't go away. All of us frequently had colds, so we didn't think much of it. But he just could not shake that cough. Brian felt something was wrong so he went back to the doctor and there was a spot on his lung. That is when they saw another tumor. After that, it went downhill quickly for him. He started losing a lot of weight.

After Brian's second operation, we had a game coming up against the Baltimore Colts on November 23, and that is when I told the rest of the team about Brian's dire condition. I spoke to the players in the locker room and told them we would dedicate the game to Brian. Unfortunately, we lost the game, 24–21, but we still gave the game ball to him at Illinois Masonic Hospital. Somehow, Brian was able to joke about the fact that we lost the game we dedicated to him.

My relationship with Brian was just a snapshot of what could be accomplished if people of different ethnic backgrounds took the time to get to truly know one another.

Brian was a very lively individual. He was the only man in the history of major college football to lead the nation in rushing and scoring and not get drafted. He didn't have a lot of speed, but he did work hard. Our relationship really developed after we started rooming together. We talked about playing the same position and we and our wives went to Chicago Blackhawks hockey games together. I miss him to this day.

In May of 2007, a Gale Sayers Roast took place in Chicago, with Hall of Famers Lem Barney, Deacon Jones, Merlin Olsen, and Dick Butkus taking part. Dave Mann, the executive director of the Gale Sayers Center, also organized a 36th-anniversary *Brian's Song* reunion for the fall of 2007. The event will bring together the cast members from the movie for the first time since it was produced in 1971.

The funds from the roast and the reunion will be used to benefit the Gale Sayers Center, which will assist in the

Somehow, Brian was able to joke about the fact that we lost the game we dedicated to him.

education and mentoring of young people. I think Brian would be proud that I am striving to improve the lives of young people today.

Greg Cote, a sportswriter for the *Miami Herald*, wrote about the Brian Piccolo Cancer Fund Drive that still thrives as a charitable event every year at Wake Forest. Cote wrote that the charity is student-initiated and run, meaning those kids were born after Piccolo died.

Cote also stated that in its 26 years the fund has generated some $750,000 from humble money-making events such as bake sales, with every penny going for cancer treatment and research at the university's Bowman Gray School of Medicine. Millions more for cancer research have been raised in Piccolo's name through a fund established by the Bears and through annual donations by the NFL, partly through player fines.

The first check, in 1980, was for a modest $3,500. Now the annual checks top $50,000, presented during halftime of an ACC basketball game on campus. Fraternities, sororities, and other campus groups join forces throughout the fall to stage fund-raising golf tournaments, dance-a-thons, silent auctions, and other events. In 2006, fund-raisers included a football team strength contest called "Pump Up for Piccolo," a walk-a-thon called "Hit the Bricks for Brian," and a showing of *Brian's Song*.

A campus residence hall bears Piccolo's name, and all incoming freshmen are shown *Brian's Song*.

"It's a live presence," Wake Forest administrator Kevin Cox was quoted as saying about Piccolo. "He's still a strong figure on campus."

Ed McCaskey, Virginia's late husband, visited Piccolo days before he died. But it was Piccolo who ended up consoling McCaskey, saying: "Don't worry, Big Ed. I'm not afraid of anything. Only [Packers linebacker Ray] Nitschke."

Ross Griffith, then a tennis player and classmate and friend of Piccolo's, recalled in that *Miami Herald* column that when Wake Forest was between head coaches following the 1963 season, Piccolo had taken it upon himself to help recruit black players. Griffith recalls that Piccolo invited local black high school athletes to visit campus, leading directly to three entering in the fall of 1964—and making Wake Forest only the second racially integrated football team (after Maryland) in the ACC.

"His personality was such that he drew people to him. He considered you a friend because of who you were, not what you looked like."

"Each day, every single day, something happens," Joy Piccolo said of his legacy and the funds it generates for cancer research. "The tributes have been incredible, and it continues. The money raised in his name is unbelievable. We never dreamed it would have gone on this long—never, ever. We have a young man who donates $41 every year in the name of his brother. We have children who have a lemonade stand and send us $12. Brian was a good person. He cared about people. He couldn't do enough for people. I think it comes back to you."

He just never got too enamored with himself. His success in football was far outweighed by the person he was.

Joy told a story last year that she hadn't told before. Brian had a receding hairline, was going bald prematurely, and it drove him crazy. He wore a toupee for a while, once to visit a seriously ill child in a hospital—a child whose own hair was lost to chemotherapy.

"After that, he threw the toupee in the garbage," Joy said. "He said, 'How could I be so vain?'"

Traci Piccolo Dolby, 39, their middle daughter, was a toddler when Brian died. "His personality was such that he drew people to him. He considered you a friend because of who you were, not what you looked like," said Traci. "Nobody ever thought my dad was good enough to do anything he accomplished. He was the consummate underdog. So many of us can relate to that and are inspired by it."

Traci, who also is a Wake Forest grad, added: "People only have the most wonderful things to say about him. It makes me so proud, and at the same time a little envious. You can feel like you were cheated. I do have those woe-is-me moments, typically like at Christmastime. I look at my kids, especially my boys, and think how neat it would be to have his influence in their lives. But my mom says there was a reason, and to look at everything we've been able to accomplish in his memory. He lives on through so many people and things. He's all around us."

Traci said she goes to Bears games and sees a few No. 41 jerseys in the crowd. She said she always makes a point to walk up to the person and say, "Nice jersey." Then she always walks away smiling.

Last Christmas she received a card from an old family friend who wrote on it, "You remind me so much of your dad." She cried.

"It was almost like having a little bit of his approval," she said.

Dan Arnold, a dentist in Lauderdale-by-the-Sea, was a high school teammate of Brian's. Arnold was quoted in the *Miami Herald* article as saying: "The timing of the black and white issue in America, the Bears putting Gale and Brian together . . . but also it was Brian finally getting to the pinnacle he was striving for, and having it jerked away from him. It's such a classic tragedy. It will last forever."

Bill Slater may have been Piccolo's best buddy growing up in Fort Lauderdale. They knew each other since first grade and played ball together in high school and at Wake Forest.

"Brian was a nice athlete but a hell of a person," said Slater. "That's what people remember. There were cliques then, but Pick didn't care if you were popular or not, dressed nice or not. You'd ask, 'Why are you running around with so-and-so?' He'd look at you like you were dumb. It didn't resonate with him. He just never got too enamored with himself. His success in football was far outweighed by the person he was. He always had a pat on the back for you, and a smile. He didn't have any bad days."

4

The Joy of Six

AS I LOOK BACK ON MY PRO FOOTBALL CAREER, I REALIZE I must have really had a chip on my shoulder in 1965. Despite all of my college football accolades, I guess I felt as if I had something to prove at the next level.

Most people today seem to associate me with the time I scored six touchdowns for the Bears against the San Francisco 49ers on December 12, 1965. But there were several incidents leading up to that record-setting day that were rather challenging. Sure, the Bears selected me as the fourth pick on the first round of the NFL draft in '65. And I was chosen to play in several College All-Star Games that year, including the East-West Shrine game, the Hula Bowl, the All-America Game, and the College All-Star Game.

Roger Staubach, the Heisman Trophy–winning quarterback from Navy, was the MVP of that East-West Shrine Game, as I recall. It was a chilly and rainy day in San Francisco. Staubach would wind up fulfilling his four-year military obligation after his senior year at the Naval Academy before joining the NFL as a 27-year-old rookie.

The Dallas Cowboys had faith that he would be worth waiting for, and man, were they right. He ended up leading Dallas to two Super Bowl wins on his way to the Hall of Fame.

Despite all of my college football accolades, I guess I felt as if I had something to prove at the next level.

Following that game, I traveled to Hawaii for the Hula Bowl. The weather was much better and so was my performance. I rushed for about 120 yards, but Larry Elkins of Baylor picked up the MVP hardware as a receiver.

It was in June of 1965 that I met up with Dick Butkus in the All-American Game in Buffalo. Butkus, out of Illinois, played for the East in that contest and I represented the West. That was the first opportunity I had to see up close and personal just what a fantastic, intimidating player Butkus was. He was physical, athletic, and relentless as a defender. His assignment was to key in on me throughout the game, and his presence was always felt. I ended up scoring one touchdown in that game. Meanwhile, Ken Willard, who picked up about 150 yards, was the game's MVP.

Willard, who starred at North Carolina, would wind up being the second player taken in the 1965 NFL draft by the San Francisco 49ers, ahead of both Butkus and me. He played nine seasons as a fullback in the NFL with the 49ers and one with the St. Louis Cardinals.

In addition to being an excellent football player, Willard was a terrific baseball prospect. He was selected in the first round of the major league draft twice, but opted to play professional football.

The All-Star Game that left me really wanting to prove myself to my doubters was the College All-Star Game, which used to be held at Soldier Field in Chicago. Before that game, I attended a special 10-day workout for all of the Bears rookies. I remember how gracious and encouraging Coach Halas was to me at that time. "How are you doing?" he asked. "Good to have you here."

Shortly thereafter, Butkus and I had to head over to the College All-Star Game practices that were held at Northwestern University in Evanston, Illinois. Back then, the top college seniors would face the defending NFL champion each year. It was sort of a kickoff to the football season and huge crowds would attend.

The game was a really big deal and full of tradition. The players were made aware of the history of the game after being selected. The first College All-Star Game was held in 1934 and it was the brainchild of sports editor Arch Ward of the *Chicago Tribune*. The game was played annually through 1976 and raised something like $4 million for Chicago charities. Most of the games were played at Soldier Field, but two were played at Northwestern. An NFL players' strike in 1974 caused the cancellation of the game that year.

The last College All-Star Game was played in 1976 against the Pittsburgh Steelers. The Super Bowl X champions were leading 24–0 when lightning and thunderstorms descended, making conditions unsafe for players and fans. Rowdy fans tore down the goal posts after players were ordered to leave the field. After the game was called, Chicago Tribune Charities chose not to resume the contests in 1977.

The series ended with the NFL champions winning 31 games and the College All-Stars nine. There were two ties.

Our college crop in 1965 included some great players and several future Pro Football Hall of Famers. Players such as Staubach, Butkus, Willard, Bob Hayes, Craig Morton, Junior Coffey, Fred Biletnikoff, Tucker Fredrickson, and Jack Snow were on that squad.

Staubach talked about how important the 1965 College All-Star Game was to his burgeoning NFL career in a *Chicago Tribune* interview. "The scouts realized that I was not just a college player; I had a strong arm. I think those couple of weeks working out there convinced Dallas and Kansas City to draft me in case I would ever leave the service," said Staubach. "It turned out great. We lost to the Browns in that All-Star Game, 24–16. I hurt my left shoulder in that game when Galen Fisk hit me in the second quarter. But in those couple of weeks the scouts saw I could be an NFL quarterback."

Part of our preparation that week leading to the game involved a scrimmage against the Bears in Rensselaer, Indiana. On the very first play of the scrimmage, I threw a block for Willard, who was playing fullback. Somehow he kicked my right leg as he tried to run past me.

I came out of the scrimmage immediately as I tried to determine if I had a sprained knee or a deep bruise or whatever. I tried running along the sideline, very gingerly. The coach for the College All-Stars that year was Otto Graham, the Hall of Fame quarterback who had starred for the Cleveland Browns. I told Coach Graham that I was able to run straight ahead, but I was unable to make cuts. I had the leg checked the next day and doctors were unable to pinpoint anything specifically wrong with it. But I just knew that I was not feeling a hundred percent and I was unable to perform the way I had become accustomed.

He was physical, athletic, and relentless as a defender. His assignment was to key in on me throughout the game, and his presence was always felt.

When I returned to the College All-Star training sessions, I did not practice for a couple of days because of the soreness in the leg. As the date of the big game approached, the annual banquet was held to showcase the All-Stars. By then, the word got to me that Graham had soured on me and thought I was faking the injury.

It was after that banquet that I decided to confront him. "Is it true that you think I am dogging it, that I am not hurt?"

Graham's eyes never met mine as he said, "That's right. I don't think you're hurt."

Graham explained that because I had been sent to the doctors and they could not find anything structurally wrong with my leg that I must be faking injury. Those comments really insulted me and got under my skin.

By the time the actual game rolled around, my leg was feeling well enough to play and I made sure Graham knew that. But he chose to keep me on the bench that entire rainy night.

The next day, all of the Chicago newspapers carried stories quoting Graham as saying: "This boy has great natural talent. But unless he changes his attitude, he'll never make the Bears, because George Halas won't have him."

That assessment just crushed me. It was the first time in my life that I had a coach come out and say he was disappointed in my work ethic and attitude.

That assessment just crushed me. It was the first time in my life that I had a coach come out and say he was disappointed in my work ethic and attitude.

I certainly respected Graham as a terrific football player. The Browns won four straight All-America Football Conference titles and had a 52–4–3 record with him at quarterback. Graham grew up in Waukegan, Illinois, and attended Northwestern, so it probably was especially important to him to show that he was in control of this College All-Star team.

Fortunately, I had a professional football career to look forward to and an opportunity to prove Graham wrong. I drove down to Rensselaer to join the Bears' training camp and Coach Halas immediately tried to put my mind at ease.

Halas said to me, "Forget about the All-Star Game; don't even worry about it. Maybe it's better you didn't play in it, anyway. I'm going to judge you by what you do here in camp. That's all."

That was so reassuring to hear. But I still felt as if I had something to prove to him and my new teammates, especially the veterans who are always prone to giving the rookies a hard time.

The Bears organization never supported any type of a formal hazing ritual for its rookies. But there were individual veterans who imposed their will, shall we say, on the new guys. The veterans, for instance, would always make sure to get the rookies drunk at least one night during training camp.

Doug Atkins was winding up his Hall of Fame career with the Bears when I arrived, before he was traded to New Orleans. Atkins, who was from Tennessee, would always have a stash of 110-proof Fighting Cock Whiskey on hand. At 6′8″, 280 pounds, Atkins had no trouble making us chug that whiskey that would burn our throats. Mighty strong stuff, indeed!

I felt certain other veterans on the team were somewhat skeptical of me at first, and perhaps some felt their roster spots were in jeopardy because of the arrival of Butkus and me as first-round draft picks. I would say it was the third exhibition game that year before many of the veterans felt I was worthy of so much of the hype that had been directed toward me in the media.

We were playing a preseason game against the Rams in Nashville, Tennessee, and we had a 7–0 lead. The Rams punted the ball to me at our 23-yard line. I made a quick maneuver with my feet and ran along the sideline on a 77-yard return for a touchdown.

In that same game, I had a 93-yard kickoff return for a score. For good measure, I threw an option pass to Dick Gordon for a third TD as we beat the Rams 28–14.

I distinctly remember defensive end Ed O'Bradovich, one of those veterans who might have questioned me in the beginning, coming up to me after the game and simply smiling. His smile of approval made me start feeling like part of the team, like I really belonged.

During training camp my rookie year, I began to survey my competition on the team. Jon Arnett, for one, was a veteran who had a fine NFL career, mostly with the Rams. The former All-American from Southern Cal was great at finding a hole and darting through it. At 5′11″, 200 pounds, Arnett had the balance of an outstanding acrobat. But he had been in the league 10 years already and his body had taken a beating. So I figured I would soon be able to supplant him.

It was time for the regular season to start and we were trounced by the San Francisco 49ers by the score of 52–24. I had just one carry in my pro debut. We also lost our second game, this time 30–28, in Los Angeles. I carried the ball just once again, but this time I scored a touchdown.

I am left-handed, so I rolled out to my left on a play that was supposed to be an option pass, just like the one I threw to Gordon in the preseason game. Gordon must have been covered that time, so I reversed my field with the ball and ran 18 yards for the score. It wasn't exactly the way the play was drawn up, but Coach Halas could not complain about the result.

Perhaps it was that play that gave Halas the confidence to insert me in the starting lineup for the first time in the third game of the year against the Green Bay Packers. I didn't know that I was going to start until right before the game. We were in the locker room in Green Bay when Halas yelled out the starting lineup. When I heard him say "Sayers at halfback," I was stunned. We lost our third straight by the score of 23–14, but I knew I had won the starting job. I scored on a six-yard run and I caught a 65-yard TD pass from Rudy Bukich. I had five catches on the afternoon, and 80 yards rushing on 17 carries.

I felt certain other veterans on the team were somewhat skeptical of me at first, and perhaps some felt their roster spots were in jeopardy...

The next week, we played the Rams, this time at Wrigley Field, and I knew ahead of time that I was going to start. That really made me nervous and it began an unpleasant ritual of throwing up before the start of every game.

It was our home opener that year—my first time to perform in front of the Bears fans during the regular season. It was an inauspicious start on the ground that day for me. I gained just 12 yards on nine carries. But I did catch a screen pass and maneuver 80 yards for a touchdown.

Following that game, 300-pound Rosey Grier of the Rams offered a flattering quote to the reporters regarding my touchdown reception and run. "I hit him so hard, I thought my shoulder must have busted him in two," said Grier. "I heard a roar from the crowd and figured he had fumbled, so I started scrambling around looking for the loose ball. But there was no ball, and Sayers was gone."

Later in that same game, I threw another option pass to Gordon for a 26-yard touchdown as we won our first game of the season, 31–6.

I distinctly remember defensive end Ed O'Bradovich, one of those veterans who might have questioned me in the beginning, coming up to me after the game and simply smiling.

With the threat of running or passing when I carried the ball to my left, it prevented defensive backs from always coming up quickly to try to stop me on the sweeps. It was an ingenious strategy deployed by Halas and it certainly made me more effective.

I was beginning to learn the nuances of the professional game, realizing that the players were bigger and faster than most of those I had played against in college. But the game itself was basically the same for me.

Still, there remained skeptics around the league who thought I was a flash in the pan. We had a game against the Vikings coming up and their coach, Norm Van Brocklin, said something to his local reporters to the effect that he thought I was just another speedy little back, nothing special.

Van Brocklin told the reporters that I had not really been hit hard yet and he thought my roommate, Andy Livingston, was actually the better back. That was all I needed to hear to provide extra incentive to face the Vikings that year. I scored four touchdowns in the second half of that game, which seesawed back and forth.

The Vikings retook the lead in that game, 37–31, with just two minutes left. Fred Cox kicked off and I took it at our 4-yard line. A wedge of blockers opened up a hole on the left side and I went 96 yards untouched. I didn't want any clipping penalties, so I remember looking back and yelling to my teammates, "Don't block, don't block!"

We would add another score after Butkus intercepted a pass and took it to the Vikings' 11. A few plays later, I took it into the end zone and we won, 45–37.

After that game, cocaptains Bob Wetoska, Mike Ditka, and Mike Pyle presented me with the game ball. The whole team gathered around me and sang the traditional, "Hooray for Sayers, he's a horse's ass!"

I felt like a horse's rear end after the Detroit Lions game the following week, even though we won. I took my hardest hit of the season in that game when Wally Hilgenberg clotheslined me along the sideline. I must have been looking the other way when his elbow caught me under my chin and sent me reeling.

Our best team effort came the next

"I hit him so hard, I thought my shoulder must have busted him in two."

—Rosey Grier

week in a rematch with the Packers, who came in with a six-game winning streak. We upset them 31–10. I ran for one touchdown from 10 yards out and returned a punt 62 yards. I got dragged down at the 15.

My first 100-yard rushing game came against the Giants when I had 113 yards. We lost a disputed game to Baltimore, 26–21, and then beat St. Louis (34–13), Detroit (17–10), and the Giants (35–14). That's when I scored my 13th and 14th touchdowns of the season, which was then the NFL record for rookies. I would wind up with 22 touchdowns in 14 games, which is still the NFL rookie record.

We traveled to Baltimore for a rematch with the Colts and won 13–0 as I rushed for 118 yards and our defense did the rest. That set the stage for my signature game against the 49ers at Wrigley Field. It was the next-to-last game of the season and my mentor and advisor, Buddy Young, gave me a call at home the night before.

Van Brocklin told the reporters that I had not really been hit hard yet and he thought my roommate, Andy Livingston, was actually the better back.

"You got a shot at Rookie of the Year," he said. "But they're pushing Bob Hayes and Tucker Fredrickson. You have to have a good day against San Francisco."

But even I could not have predicted the kind of day I wound up having. My six touchdowns tied an NFL record and I set a single-game record of 336 total yards. Young called me back that night and said, "I wanted you to have a good day, but not that good a day. That was ridiculous."

It was a great day for me, but I still considered the four-touchdown performance against the Vikings more impressive because it meant the difference in a close game. We walloped the 49ers 61–20 that day, scoring at will, it seemed. The outcome was never in doubt, unlike at the Vikings game.

I remember that Coach Halas had us wear longer nylon cleats for that 49ers game because it had rained hard the day before and the field was a muddy quagmire. Despite the condition of the field, I generally had no trouble cutting on it.

My first score came on a screen pass from Bukich from our own 20-yard line. There were a bunch of 49ers around me when I made the catch, but I spotted that 18 inches of daylight that I require and made my way for the TD. That was the most difficult touchdown of the day for me because I had to maneuver past several defenders.

My second, third, and fourth touchdowns came on sweeps where the blocking was crisp and efficient and I simply sprinted in for the scores. My fifth touchdown came from close range on a one-yard plunge.

Then the degree of difficulty increased. Midway through the fourth period the 49ers' Tommy Davis punted to me at our 15-yard line. I caught the low line drive and made a quick move to elude the first wave of tacklers. The only 49er to touch me the rest of the route was Ken Willard, who was chasing me. I shook him off my leg and I was on my way.

Young called me back that night and said, "I wanted you to have a good day, but not that good a day. That was ridiculous."

At the end of that run, I guess I got a little full of myself. Generally, I would simply give the ball to the referee after a score. You know, act like you have been there before. But after scoring my sixth TD I threw the football into the air and did a little dance shuffle with my feet. Maybe it was a rendition of the "Run Around" dance I learned in high school. I am not sure. But it was nothing contrived like so many of the touchdown dances you see players performing today. Mine was just an uncharacteristic, spontaneous reaction.

I might have had a chance for a seventh touchdown when we advanced to the 49ers' 2-yard line late in the game. But Halas had already taken me out of the game with such a big lead. I had no problem with that, even though the Wrigley Field fans began chanting, "We want Sayers! We want Sayers!"

Just think, if I hadn't slipped, and if I had just another 18 inches of daylight… maybe I could have scored my seventh touchdown.

Arnett was in the game and he scored the final TD of the afternoon.

My six touchdowns in that game tied the record set by the Chicago Cardinals' Ernie Nevers on November 28, 1929. According to my research, Nevers, who was a fullback, scored all 40 of the Cardinals' points in a 40–6 rout of the Bears that year. In addition to the six touchdowns, Nevers added four extra points.

The previous game, Nevers had also scored all of the Cardinals' points—19. The Pro Football Hall of Famer was often compared to the legendary Jim Thorpe because of his multiple abilities to run, pass, and kick.

Actually, Halas sent me back in to that 1965 game against the 49ers for a punt return on the very last play of the game. I caught Davis's punt on our 19 and saw a bit of daylight. My blockers had opened up a lane to the left, then I cut back and slipped a little bit before they dragged me down.

Just think, if I hadn't slipped, and if I had just another 18 inches of daylight…maybe I could have scored my seventh touchdown.

5

Testing My Resolve

WHEN I FIRST CAME TO THE BEARS IN 1965, WE ALSO had rookies Jimmy Jones out of Wisconsin and Dick Gordon out of Michigan State as new members of the offense. They were both outstanding wide receivers, and they were trying to make the team too. So they were always running full speed like me. For the most part, I think I had a good relationship with everybody on the field on both sides of the ball. And the black and white players on our team got along just fine. You don't usually see that kind of problem in sports. There might have been racial problems with other people in Chicago 15 blocks down the street from where we were practicing, but not there on the field. The number one concern with the players on our team was whether a guy could help us win football games. We were all there for one cause, and that was to win.

I remember playing in an exhibition game in Nashville, Tennessee, and we all heard the "N" word from fans throughout the game. That preseason game in 1965 was against the Los Angeles Rams. I scored on a 97-yard kickoff return, scored again on a 65-yard punt return, and then threw a touchdown pass on a halfback option play. But that type of name-calling never affected us as black players. There was too much else going on in terms of racial turbulence in the 1960s with the riots and Dr. Martin Luther King preaching nonviolence.

We had a lot of older players on our team in my rookie year, and maybe they had a right to fear that we were going to take their jobs. Dick Butkus took Bill George's job in 1965. I took someone's job. So the veterans had to be a little afraid. My hope was that the presence of so many very good young players would make the veterans play better, and thereby make the whole team better. But there was probably some animosity from some of the veterans toward the rookies.

The strength of all of our relationships was certainly tested in 1969, when we finished 1–13 for the worst record in franchise history. I remember receiving a letter from some guy before that season. He said: "The reason you got hurt was because you let your hair grow." Even though I had let my hair grow out the year I got hurt, I doubt that had anything to do with our record.

It was just a bizarre year all around. In fact, it was during that season Coach Halas's secretary, Miss Frances Osborn, jumped out of a 26th-floor window. She had been his secretary for about 30 years and I guess she had suffered a stroke six months before her suicide. The stroke had affected her speech and obviously left her extremely depressed.

It was also in 1969 that Brian Piccolo was operated on for the malignant tumor in his chest. Another running back teammate, Ronnie Bull, tore up his knee in '69. And our number one draft pick, 21-year-old lineman Rufus Mayes, was hospitalized for a bleeding ulcer.

As the losses piled up that year, many sportswriters and commentators began taking shots at me, writing and saying that I was not the same runner that I was before my devastating knee injury.

One headline read: "Let's Face It, Gale Sayers Is Not the Gale Sayers of Old." And another headline said: "Bear Fact: Sayers Is Not Performing as a 'Gale Force.'"

That's when Coach Halas called me into his office to ease my mind. He told me not to be upset and bothered about what people wrote or said. "Just go out and run like you have been running," he said.

My hope was that the presence of so many very good young players would make the veterans play better...

After the first five games of the 1969 season, I had rushed for only 220 yards on 68 attempts for a 3.2 yards average. I ranked 16th among NFL runners at that point, not exactly up to my standards.

The Chicago media continued to question whether the knee surgery had robbed me of my ability to cut and run with the burst that had become my signature. I remember Dr. Fox getting into a heated argument with a writer about my physical condition. Dr. Fox wound up yelling at the writer and telling him that he was going to "eat those words."

After that encounter, Dr. Fox had a very blunt, face-to-face conversation with me about my knee. He told me that I still possessed the same God-given talent that I had before I injured my knee in 1968. He told me that I was thinking too much on the field instead of doing things instinctively, as I had always done since the time I started playing football as a little kid. He said, "Stop thinking and just go out and do your thing!"

Initially, I had doubts about my ability to run like that again. But it was a conversation with Brian that really set me straight. He knew that talking about my knee injury was a touchy topic with me. But one day he broached the subject and offered his opinion, which I valued. First he acknowledged how difficult it must have been for me to hear all those suggestions and criticisms I was receiving from all quarters. But he added that he felt I was a bit hesitant when I approached the hole, almost as if I was trying to wait a split second so I could break every run for a long touchdown. He thought that I was so anxious to prove my critics wrong that I tried to make every run a long scoring jaunt.

> *He said, "Stop thinking and just go out and do your thing!"*

Brian said that I should simply try to hit the hole faster. At first I became a little angry at Brian. But then I figured maybe Pick had a point. Brian lightened the mood when he threatened to call the mafia to take care of my other knee. We had a good laugh and I started to take his advice to heart.

Brian and I had worked out together a lot between the 1968 and '69 seasons while I was rehabbing my knee.

He would always make jokes about being able to beat me running in training camp. And he would make jokes about the scar on my knee following the surgery.

The fact that I was able to sort of reinvent myself as a runner in 1969 and gain more than 1,000 yards in a 14-game season made me feel especially proud, even though we suffered through a miserable season as a team.

• • •

The best quarterback that I ever had was Rudy Bukich in my rookie year. Rudy had a rifle arm and we called him "Rifle Rudy." He was tough. Now Bill Wade…it seemed like he was probably 50 when he came to the Bears. Actually he was 35 but clearly on the downside of his career after helping the Bears win the NFL title in 1963.

Wade had been a first-round draft pick of the Los Angeles Rams in 1952 out of Vanderbilt. And he was a two-time Pro Bowl selection in 1958 and 1963. But he wound up his career with more interceptions—134—than touchdowns—124. By the time I joined the Bears, it was his time to go and Rudy took over for him. Bill Wade came back in 1966, but he retired after that season.

Brian said that I should simply try to hit the hole faster. At first I became a little angry at Brian. But then I figured maybe Pick had a point.

Then in my third year with the Bears, young Kent Nix and Larry Rakestraw were in that mix of new quarterbacks we tried. Then it was Virgil Carter, Jack Concannon,

Bobby Douglass, and maybe one or two more. It just seemed as though, when I was playing, we changed quarterbacks every game because nobody could do anything. We didn't have enough good football players to win a championship. We went 9–5 in 1965 and after that we went downhill.

In '65 Dick Gordon, Jimmy Jones, Dick Butkus, and I joined the team, along with Ralph Kurek out of Wisconsin. In succeeding years, it is hard to remember who we drafted in the first round. Rufus Mayes, a lineman out of Ohio State, was our number one pick in 1969. Bobby Douglass was our second-round choice that year.

Douglass came out of the University of Kansas and was a good athlete, but he had no touch with his passes whatsoever. He was a freshman at Kansas when I was a senior. If you were five yards away from him, he would throw the ball as hard as he could at you. And if you were 35 yards down the field, he would fire it to you at the same speed. Douglass was a running quarterback who gained 968 yards in 1972, and back then you couldn't win with a running quarterback.

Douglass threw the ball so hard that he had his Bears teammates ducking in practice, because they didn't want to get hit by the ball, especially on a really cold day when he would practically break your fingers with the ball.

In 1966 our first-round draft pick was a guy named George Rice out of Louisiana State, in 1967 it was Loyd Phillips out of Arkansas, and in 1968 it was Mike Hull out of USC. None of those guys made a major impact with the Bears.

We tied Pittsburgh for the worst record in the NFL in 1969. It was after that horrible season that we lost the coin flip for the number one overall pick and the Steelers took Terry Bradshaw out of Louisiana Tech. Of course, it was Bradshaw who led them to all those Super Bowls.

To have a Butkus and Sayers on our team—if we had had anything—we should have won a championship. It is just that a lot of those players got old quickly on our team—guys like Rosey Taylor and Bennie McRae, Stan Jones, Richie Petitbon, Davey Whitsell, Bill George, and Doug Atkins. A lot of those guys had been great football players and they hung around a few more years because they won the title in 1963. We had three or four Hall of Famers there, but they couldn't play anymore. After those guys got old, we simply did not pick up enough good football players in the draft.

But there are times when I wonder how much more effective I could have been as a running back if we had been fortunate enough to have a steady, more reliable quarterback situation during my career.

I have never been a selfish player and the individual stats don't mean nearly as much to me since we were unable to win a title during my career. But there are times when I wonder how much more effective I could have been as a running back if we had been fortunate enough to have a steady, more reliable quarterback situation during my career.

I mean, the Packers had Hall of Fame quarterback Bart Starr to help take the pressure off Paul Hornung and Jim

Taylor so they could be more effective running the football. The same was true with the Baltimore Colts, who were in our Western Division at that time. The Colts had Hall of Fame quarterback Johnny Unitas in the mid-1960s. That gave players like Lenny Moore and Alan Ameche more ways to be effective offensively.

The defensive teams did not have to be geniuses to realize that I was going to get the ball, and that I was probably going to run to the wide side of the field...

Even in the 1980s, Walter Payton had Jim McMahon quarterbacking the Bears; and Emmitt Smith had Troy Aikman at quarterback for the Dallas Cowboys. You have to have more than one offensive weapon to be an effective threat.

Other teams knew that our offense was going to be "Gale Right" or "Gale Left." Opposing defenses were able to key on me almost exclusively, realizing that our quarterback—for the most part—was not going to present a major threat to them.

That situation was made even more difficult for me back then because of the location of the hash marks in the NFL. They were much wider in the '60s and '70s than they are now, so you had a short side of the field and a wide side of the field when the ball was positioned on one of the hash marks. The defensive teams did not have to be geniuses to realize that I was going to get the ball, and that I was probably going to run to the wide side of the field, where I had more room to navigate. So the defenses were set up to stop me on the wide side. I could not set out to run to the short side of the field; that

That's me in the back row, wearing No. 30 this time. We won two straight championships at Howard Kennedy Grade School in Omaha. I scored about 27 touchdowns this season and we beat Boys Town for the title, 39–0. I scored five touchdowns in that game.

Kansas had recruited me as a defensive player—a linebacker or defensive back. When we first started working out my freshman year, there seemed to be a lack of willing running backs; that is when the coaches started taking a look at me.

I rushed for 941 yards in 10 games during my junior year at Kansas. I became the first back in Big Eight history to reach 2,000 career yards at that point. Freshmen were not allowed to play on the varsity at major colleges back then.
COURTESY OF AP/WIDE WORLD PHOTOS.

Posing for my official photo with a college All-Star game uniform on. It was probably the only time I smiled all week. Coach Otto Graham thought I was faking an injury earlier in the week and refused to let me play in the game at Soldier Field in 1965 COURTESY OF AP/ WIDE WORLD PHOTOS.

Scoring my sixth touchdown against the San Francisco 49ers at Wrigley Field on December 12, 1965, is something I will never forget. I was not trying to showboat as I headed for the end zone. I just couldn't believe how easy it seemed for me that day.

I had worn No. 48 all through high school. As a freshman at Kansas, I was given No. 47. When I made the varsity, I got No. 48 back. As a member of the Bears, as shown here, I got the No. 40 jersey because incumbent running back Andy Livingston owned No. 48.

I always loved playing against the Green Bay Packers. George Halas inserted me in the starting lineup for the first time in the third game of my rookie year against Green Bay. I didn't know that I was going to start until right before the game. We lost our third straight game by the score of 23–14, but I knew I had won the starting job. I scored on a six-yard run and I caught a 65-yard TD pass from Rudy Bukich. I had five catches on the afternoon, and 80 yards rushing on 17 carries.

Top: Dick Butkus joined the Bears as a first-round draft pick in 1965, the same year I joined the team. He was elected to the Pro Football Hall of Fame in 1979, his first year of eligibility. We remain great friends and have so many shared memories.

Bottom: I have run into so many fans who claimed to have been at Wrigley Field when I scored six touchdowns against the 49ers in 1965. There must have been 200,000 people in attendance instead of less than 40,000 reported, or so it seems.

While scoring six touchdowns in a game my rookie year may have been spectacular, the game that meant the most to me that year was against the Vikings. I scored four touchdowns in the second half of a seesaw game that we won 45–37.

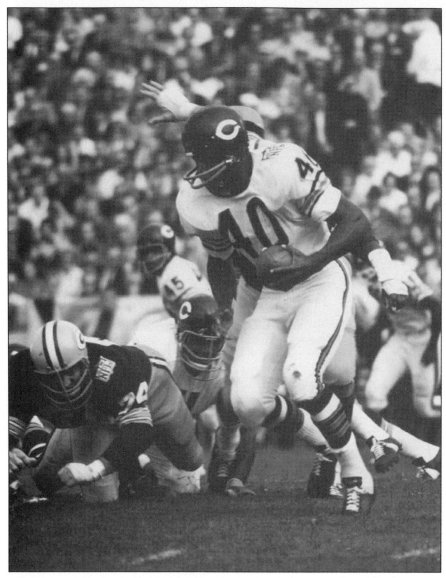

When you get to this level, I think the only thing an NFL running back has to be aware of is that he has so many more plays. I honestly don't think a coach can teach you how to run. He can teach you blocking techniques. But as far as running...I don't think so. It is difficult to change a back's running style.

This was the shortest of my six touchdowns on Dec. 12, 1965 against the San Francisco 49ers at muddy Wrigley Field. If I had known that the six touchdown performance would have been such a memorable deal even today, I would have maybe scored two or three more.

I always felt there was no way one man could stop me in the open field. Here I am sizing up two defenders on the Rams at Wrigley Field.

With the threat of running or passing when I carried the ball to my left, it prevented defensive backs from always coming up quickly to try to stop me on the sweeps. It was an ingenious strategy deployed by Halas and it certainly made me more effective.

The kick returns gave me an opportunity to touch the ball many more times. The Bears wanted me back there returning kicks and I wanted to be there. I was never frightened, even though I knew there were 11 defenders running full speed toward me, ready to rip my head off. COURTESY OF AP/WIDE WORLD PHOTOS.

When it came to running the football from scrimmage, most of the Bears offensive linemen knew that all they had to do was get in the way of somebody and I could find daylight.

No one had ever taught me anything about running the football—maybe a coach reminded me about changing hands with the football to make sure it was on the outside toward the sideline in case of a fumble. But other than that, everything pretty much came naturally to me. COURTESY OF AP/WIDE WORLD PHOTOS.

I had some of my most memorable games against the Minnesota Vikings. This was one of my few short runs against them at Wrigley Field.

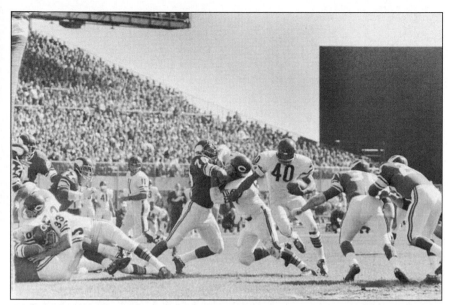

We beat the Vikings 45–37 in my rookie year after I scored four touchdowns in the second half. After that game, cocaptains Bob Wetoska, Mike Ditka, and Mike Pyle presented me with the game ball. The whole team gathered around me and sang the traditional, "Hooray for Sayers, he's a horse's ass!"

COURTESY OF AP/WIDE WORLD PHOTOS.

As long as it wasn't snowing and freezing cold, I looked forward to playing the Vikings when their stadium was outdoors in Bloomington, Minnesota. Now that the Vikings play in the Metrodome in Minneapolis, the games are not the same.

just didn't make sense. A lot of people forget about those hash marks but they made a big difference.

Jim Brown had to deal with that, and so did a lot of other great backs. Then all of a sudden the NFL put the hash marks in the middle of the field, about the width of the goal posts, and we no longer had a short side of the field. That was really huge.

6

My Favorite Running Backs

PEOPLE CONSTANTLY ASK MY OPINION OF WHICH CURRENT and former players I consider to be the greatest running backs of all time, the ones I would pay to see play.

I am always flattered to hear my name thrown into other observers' conversations, even though injury cut short my career and limited me to 68 NFL games. The fact that I was able to make such an impression on Hall of Fame voters to induct me at the age of 34 is an honor I don't take lightly.

When I was coming along as a high school football player, my idol as a running back was Jim Brown of the Cleveland Browns. And after watching many outstanding running backs come and go over the past half-century, Brown remains at the top of my list. Why? He was the complete running back. He had good size, good speed, great quickness, and a relentless will to succeed. Despite a constant pounding from defenses that were always targeting him, he never missed a game in nine years.

Brown had great hands, making him a superb receiver out of the backfield. He also returned kickoffs, and even threw three touchdown passes.

Like so many of us running backs who came after Brown in the 1960s and '70s, he did not have the luxury of playing on AstroTurf, where his quickness could have been accentuated. He played on a lot of beat-up fields such as Municipal Stadium in Cleveland, which was shared by the Cleveland Indians baseball team. The field would often be muddy and treacherous during the winter months, yet Brown's quickness and sure-footed running style usually prevailed.

Next on my list of top running backs would be O.J. Simpson, the 1968 Heisman Trophy winner out of Southern Cal. He was a world-class sprinter in college. And when he joined the Buffalo Bills, he had an outstanding offensive line blocking for him.

O.J. had much better speed than I did. He didn't do a whole lot of juking and dodging when he ran the way I did. O.J. could just make one move and then outrun everybody.

When it comes to talking about O.J. and the legal problems he got involved in regarding the murder of his wife and her friend, I don't know if he did it or not. That is for O.J. and God to know for sure.

Barry Sanders was a runner a lot of people compared to me. He used the entire field and he had so much quickness. He could stop on a dime. He was tremendous. If he had decided to continue playing instead of retiring at the top of his game the way he did, he could have gotten

20,000 yards in his career. Just two years before he decided to retire, he gained 2,000 yards with that line blocking for him in Detroit.

Sanders ran low to the ground and rushed for more than 1,000 yards in each of his 10 seasons with the Lions (1989–1998). I was very surprised to see him retire when he did. I believe you should play as long as you can physically. You just don't quit and walk away. As an NFL running back, you have been given a gift from God. Just like a singer such as Nat King Cole or an entertainer has. You should be grateful for the gift that God has given you and you owe it to yourself, your family, and your fans to make the most of it.

O.J. could just make one move and then outrun everybody.

When I think of Earl Campbell and how he dominated as a powerfully built running back with the Houston Oilers, my first thought is that it is too bad he did not consider running around some people. He would always attempt to run over and through defenders, even though he had good speed. I think that all of the beatings he took had an effect on his health and shortened his career. But he was a terrific back and a lot of people seem to forget just how good he was.

Campbell took tremendous physical pounding throughout his career, yet he missed only six games out of 115 because of injuries. Midway into his seventh season, he was traded by the Oilers to the New Orleans Saints for a first-round draft pick. He played a season and a half with the Saints before retiring after the 1985 campaign.

It is very sad to learn that Campbell is suffering today from anxiety attacks. I cannot imagine how frightening that must be. His website tells the story of his first panic attack. According to the site, after retiring from the NFL and while working for the University of Texas, Campbell had his first attack when waiting at a stoplight as he was driving home one day. He did not know what it was and did not tell anyone. That night, another attack hit him while he was sleeping. He was rushed to the hospital but nothing wrong was found. After hiding in his bedroom for a month, Campbell reached out for help. After seeking the opinion of a second doctor, he was diagnosed with panic disorder and prescribed medication that provided relief.

I believe you should play as long as you can physically. You just don't quit and walk away.

Eric Dickerson is also on my list of top running backs, but it is too bad he did not decide to remain with the Rams. He was a big back—about 225 pounds. I weighed about 198 to 200 pounds at the start of the seasons. Then I would go down to about 190 during the season. I felt very good at that weight. But Dickerson had the size and speed combination that made him effective, although he ran with that straight-up style that made him a bigger target for tacklers. Still, they couldn't seem to bring him down until after he had picked up good yardage.

When I ran, I tried to make sure a tackler did not get a direct hit on me. I can remember maybe 10 times in my entire career when I really got nailed. One time, I remember, Atlanta Falcons' linebacker Tommy Nobis thought he had a direct shot at me. The fans thought he got me real good and they let out a roar. But Nobis knew that he didn't. He said to me, "Dammit, Gale, I missed you."

Of course, the legendary Walter Payton set so many Bears and NFL records that he cemented his legacy as one of the greatest of all time. Many people want to compare me to Payton in terms of who was the greater back for the Bears. First of all, we were totally different types of backs. Where I was constantly trying to elude tacklers in order to gain yardage, it seemed that Payton often went out of his way to run over potential tacklers. As it turned out, both of our methods worked for us in terms of gaining yardage and scoring touchdowns.

In 1985, Payton rushed for 1,551 yards, caught 49 passes, and scored 11 touchdowns. Such were the standards of excellence for the NFL's all-time leading rusher, who capped a Hall of Fame career with an appearance in Super Bowl XX in New Orleans.

Despite the personal disappointment of not having an opportunity to score a Super Bowl touchdown from close range, Payton always knew his place in Bears history. He retired holding 26 Bears records and eight NFL marks. He was voted to the Pro Bowl nine times and had his No. 34 jersey retired. Everyone who ever watched him play remembers the intangible qualities that made Payton the embodiment of perseverance, consistency, and

Earl Campbell would always attempt to run over and through defenders, even though he had good speed. I think that all of the beatings he took had an effect on his health and shortened his career.

durability. Although quarterback Jim McMahon received most of the attention for being such a vocal leader of the offense, Payton was the unit's most physically durable and reliable performer.

But Dickerson had the size and speed combination that made him effective, although he ran with that straight-up style that made him a bigger target for tacklers.

Former Bears offensive lineman Revie Sorey talked about what it was like blocking for Payton. "It was incredible," Sorey told the *Chicago Tribune*. "If you just got in the way, you made a good block. And I happened to throw a couple of 'get-in-the-way' blocks. And he made me look outstanding. Whenever we ran a sweep I figured we could get at least 10 or 15 yards. If he broke it, that was gravy. He was a guy who could do so many things. When you look at a lot of running backs today, they can't handle the punishment. You've got third-down backs now and all that sort of thing."

The Bears led the league in rushing in 1977 behind the running of Payton, and then did not lead the league in that category again until 1983. The entire offensive line of Jay Hilgenberg at center, Tom Thayer and Mark Bortz at guards, and Jim Covert and Keith Van Horne at the tackles remained intact for seven years. That continuity was extremely important to the Bears' success as a team.

Another key factor in Payton's success was the fact that his offensive linemen were able to execute their blocking strategy and techniques to perfection. Covert, a member of the College Football Hall of Fame, always talks about the differences in blocking strategies employed today, compared to in the 1980s.

"Absolutely, I see a lot of differences," Covert said in the *Chicago Tribune*. "I see that they have the biggest possible human beings they can get, and they put them on the offensive line. Then they go straight ahead. They zone block. Very rarely do you see guards pull out in space. I was a tackle and we would run those 'counter-OT' plays and I would pull seven, eight, nine times a game. Jay Hilgenberg, our center, would pull on a lot of plays. Our guards would pull a lot with the sweeps we used to run. You don't see that anymore. You just see the big guys going straight ahead. The other thing that bothers me a little bit is the way they pass protect. Nobody gets their hands up, nobody gets their head back [to block]. Nobody punches anymore. They are so big that they just sort of absorb everything."

Everyone who ever watched him play remembers the intangible qualities that made Payton the embodiment of perseverance, consistency, and durability.

Among current NFL running backs, LaDainian Tomlinson has put together some impressive numbers in his career as he continues his assault on many league records. Last February during Super Bowl Week, Tomlinson recalled watching Payton play on television. "I told my mother then that I wanted to be a football player," said Tomlinson, who was a corecipient—along with New Orleans quarterback Drew Brees—of the Walter Payton Man of the Year award. In 2006, Tomlinson broke the 46-year-old

NFL scoring record set by my friend and contemporary Paul Hornung.

A lot of people forget that Hornung once scored five touchdowns in a game against the Baltimore Colts. That accomplishment kind of got lost in the shuffle because it was the same day I scored six touchdowns against the 49ers in 1965.

The way Marcus Allen was able to smoothly follow his blockers and turn on bursts of speed while running in a fairly erect stance made him unique.

Hornung's record of 176 points in 1960 lasted longer than Babe Ruth's home-run record. And he was a terrific kicker. I recall that Hornung once converted a 52-yard free-kick field goal to beat my Bears, 13–10, in 1967.

I also had great appreciation for the way Marcus Allen ran the football. There is good reason he is a member of the Pro Football Hall of Fame. The way he was able to smoothly follow his blockers and turn on bursts of speed while running in a fairly erect stance made him unique. Perhaps his most impressive statistic was the 145 touchdowns he scored, including a then league record 123 rushing TDs.

Another thing I find remarkable about Allen's career is that he spent the first two seasons at Southern Cal as a backup to Charles White, who was a Heisman Trophy winner. When he finally became a starter, Allen rushed for 1,563 yards, which was good for second in the nation in 1980.

But his real breakthrough year was 1981, when Allen rushed for 2,342 yards, becoming the first player in NCAA history to rush for more than 2,000 yards in one season. USC has retired Allen's jersey number, and coach John Robinson called him "the greatest player I ever saw."

Another outstanding back who caught my eye before injuries took their toll on him was Priest Holmes. At 5′9″, 215 pounds, Holmes really packs a solid frame, and he ran low enough to the ground to make him a difficult target for tacklers.

Holmes came out of the University of Texas, which has produced so many great running backs over the years. In fact, Holmes played alongside future Heisman Trophy winner Ricky Williams at Texas.

Astonishingly, Holmes joined the Baltimore Ravens as an undrafted free agent in 1997. He rushed for more than 1,000 yards with the Ravens in 1998 and he helped Baltimore win Super Bowl XXXV in 2001. He signed with the Kansas City Chiefs the next year and he went on to lead the entire NFL in rushing with 1,555 yards.

7

Preparing to Quit

Near Addiction

AFTER I SUFFERED MY SECOND KNEE INJURY IN 1970, THE
Bears medical staff began giving me shots to ease the throbbing pain. I have never spoken about this publicly before, but the shots would put me to sleep for about five minutes or so, and I must confess that I really started looking forward to getting them.

Was I becoming addicted to the painkillers?

I feared I was at the time. I began looking forward to that euphoric feeling and that started to really frighten me. You hear about other people innocently becoming addicted to painkillers, but I never thought something like that could happen to me. But it slowly, insidiously was becoming habitual to me. I enjoyed it, looked forward to it. Shoot me up and put me to sleep!

With two or three shots I would probably be out for five minutes. You wake up and you feel pretty good. What was in the shots? I don't have the slightest idea. Maybe a combination of cortisone and Novocain. But the feeling was unmistakable.

No doubt about it, many other Bears players thought this was the thing to do at the time. Give me a shot and let me go out and play. As players back in the '60s and '70s, we thought this was just another way to go out and play to help the team win.

But after the game when the shots wore off, the pain in the knee often would be worse than it was before the shot.

But it slowly, insidiously was becoming habitual to me. I enjoyed it, looked forward to it. Shoot me up and put me to sleep!

What was happening to me? What damage was I doing to my body? It wasn't like the money was that great in the NFL at that time. But it was as if the teams always had that hammer over those players back then. They would say, "If you don't want to take the shot, if you don't want to play, we will get somebody else."

Painkillers of all sorts were very prevalent back then. When I started taking shots, other players on the team would come up to me and say: "Gale, have you tried this pill? Go to Dr. Fox and get one. It will make you feel great."

Thank God I had the mental strength and fortitude to resist the temptation to continue those shots and painkillers just to continue my career.

That feeling that I had when I received those shots—that feeling of lost control—was one of the major reasons I decided to retire from football. I knew I couldn't do that to my body anymore. I feel so sorry for other athletes and people in other walks of life who have been unable to walk away from this powerful force that can overtake your mind and body.

I knew during my last exhibition game against the St. Louis Cardinals in Busch Stadium in 1972 that I couldn't play anymore. Perhaps in subsequent games I could have taken some pills and taken some more shots, but I was through with doing that. I couldn't take having things done to me on the sideline to keep me on the field. It wouldn't be worth it to my body and my life after football.

That feeling that I had when I received those shots— that feeling of lost control— was one of the major reasons I decided to retire from football.

My good friend and former teammate Dick Butkus wound up suing the Bears and Dr. Theodore Fox for medical malpractice in 1975. He claimed the Bears knowingly kept him on the field with cortisone shots and other painkillers instead of having him undergo surgery on his knees. Dick was forced to retire in 1973 because of multiple knee injuries. In his lawsuit, Dick claimed the Bears would not allow him—or the rest of us players for that matter—to seek a second opinion about the condition of his knees.

Butkus agreed to take a $600,000 settlement from the Bears.

But I saw how the lawsuit created acrimony and dissension between Butkus and George Halas. In fact Butkus and the entire Bears organization seemed to be at odds for a long time. Finally, Dick was asked to join the Bears radio broadcast booth in 1985, and Butkus and I had our jersey numbers retired during a ceremony at Soldier Field in 1994.

As great a player as Dick was, how much better could he have been with today's medical technology? How much longer could he have played?

The same questions could have been asked about the longevity and quality of my career. Arthroscopic knee surgery today usually sidelines a player for a couple of months, not an entire year.

...I was often asked to do radio and television interviews. I was very shy at the time, and I usually uttered a lot of one-word answers. Looking back now, that must have surely frustrated the people interviewing me.

But both Dick and I were first-ballot Pro Football Hall of Fame selections and both of us have gone on to have very successful careers outside of football. So I try not to live in the past and wonder too much. But every now and then it is interesting to speculate.

Could I have played another year or two with the Bears if I had agreed to continue taking painkillers and shots? Hard to say. I just knew it was time for me to leave the game when I did. I had proven I could still be a major contributor to the Bears in 1969 when I returned from the devastating injury to my right knee and still managed to gain more than 1,000 yards, even though the yards may not have come in the same spectacular fashion Bears fans had become accustomed to seeing from me.

In that final game in St. Louis, I carried the ball three times and I fumbled twice. I told coach Abe Gibron at halftime that I couldn't go anymore. I knew then that it was time to move on, time to move on from football and any temporary painkillers that could adversely affect how I live my life. I believe things happen for a reason.

• • •

When I think back to my playing days, the main source of Bears coverage for fans was WGN radio in Chicago and its late Hall of Fame broadcaster Jack Brickhouse. Some games were shown on television, but nothing at all like the number of NFL games aired nowadays.

I liked Jack Brickhouse and got along well with him. He was a real "homer" and the Bears fans loved that about him. He was known for his signature expression "Hey! Hey!" Whether a Bears player scored a touchdown or a Cubs player hit a home run, Brickhouse shouted his favorite saying.

I recall Brickhouse complimenting me on running 1,000 yards in 1969 after I had rehabbed from my first knee injury. That acknowledgment really meant a lot to me.

So many people today assume that I am rich, that I made huge amounts of money during my Hall of Fame playing days. Fact is, I made a grand total of $275,000 during my seven years in the NFL.

During my first year or so in the NFL, I was often asked to do radio and television interviews. I was very shy at the time, and I usually uttered a lot of one-word answers. Looking back now, that must have surely frustrated the people interviewing me.

Coach Halas called me into his office one day and gave me some sound advice. He said, "You know, Gale, it might help you out if you took one of those courses to help you relax and speak more clearly. It will help get rid of your shyness and give you more confidence."

Having played just 68 games in the NFL, I thought there was no way I could make it to the Hall of Fame. It wasn't anything I really even gave great thought to when I was playing. Then after I had retired, I remember receiving that phone call. I was in Phoenix at the time. They told me I had been selected for the Hall of Fame.

At first I wasn't so certain it would make any difference. But I signed up anyway for one of the Dale Carnegie public speaking classes. It was amazing. It really helped me gain confidence and speak more forcefully and clearly. It was one of the best things I ever did for myself.

The Dale Carnegie Course is a self-improvement program conducted using a standardized curriculum by professional trainers throughout the world. Several variations of the course exist to assist people in sales and management. Now I can stand in front of a large group of people or sit down for a one-on-one interview and express myself confidently. What a relief!

Being prepared for life after my pro football career ended so abruptly was tremendously important. So many people today assume that I am rich, that I made huge amounts of money during my Hall of Fame playing days. Fact is, I made a grand total of

$275,000 during my seven years in the NFL. Some play-
ers today make that much in just a few games, or for one
major endorsement opportunity.

The big money in the NFL didn't start until about 1975,
when Walter Payton came into the league. But I am not
bitter about anything. I feel fortunate enough to have gotten into the NFL to accomplish what I did. The records I
set and all of the accolades in that short period of time…I
couldn't have done anything more.

Television really dictates the big money nowadays and
it is amazing how that has mushroomed the salaries of
everyone associated with the game—the players, coaches,
and team executives.

In 2004, for instance, the NFL agreed to $8 billion in
contract extensions with FOX and CBS to televise Sunday
afternoon games for six more years, deals that would also
allow the league to show better match-ups late in the season in prime time.

The current contract was worth $17.2 billion, includ-
ing the Sunday night and Monday night packages. The
extensions will run through 2011. The television money
derived from the likes of ESPN, ABC, and the other networks is extraordinary.

• • •

Having played just 68 games in the NFL, I thought there
was no way I could make it to the Hall of Fame. It wasn't
anything I really even gave great thought to when I was
playing. Then after I had retired, I remember receiving

that phone call. I was in Phoenix at the time. They told me I had been selected for the Hall of Fame. I was just 34 years old—the youngest ever to be inducted.

I was overwhelmed and just simply proud at that moment. And I am to this day. Although I had played so few games in the NFL, I guess the selection committee was impressed with the fact that I was a running back and a kick returner. No one had really seen that combination before with such success.

I asked George Halas to present me at the Hall of Fame ceremonies on July 30, 1977. What a better choice than Halas? The following is the transcript of my Hall of Fame acceptance speech:

> *Commissioner Rozelle, ladies and gentlemen. I am deeply honored to be inducted today into the NFL Hall of Fame. For anyone who has ever played football, this is the highest recognition that can be bestowed and I am both honored and grateful for this recognition.*
>
> *Most people of my generation refuse to acknowledge or give credit to others who have helped them in life. I am being enshrined because of my physical ability and because of my team-mates. But there is another side to a professional football player, and that is to stay mentally alert in a case of a physical injury that might shorten your career. By being mentally afloat, I meant to seek out all-season job opportunities when I came to the game. I did from the start. In my*

first three years, I had job opportunities from two companies. It kept me mentally afloat and gave me the incentive to go back to school and finish my undergraduate degree and my master's degree. It brings to mind what I was all about in the first place. I went to college not as an athletic student, but a student-athlete.

No one can get here alone, however. So I want to express my thanks to a few people who have made it possible for me to be here today. I want to say a special thanks to my high school coach, Frank Smagacz. It was he who really got me started in football. He taught me the fundamentals and helped give direction to my life. I am now and always will be deeply indebted to him. I want to give thanks to my college coach, Jack Mitchell. Coach Mitchell recruited me to the University of Kansas and became not only my coach but also a very personal friend.

And I want to give a special thanks to George Halas, a man who more than anyone else has made professional football what it is today. There is not much you can say about someone who has become a legend in his own lifetime, but I want to try. Mr. Halas is one of those rare individuals who is not content with things as they are, but sees the way they could be and works to make things better. I cannot thank him enough for all he has done for me and my family and the many other National Football League players he has touched.

And finally, I want to thank the many people I played with in the NFL, teammates and opponents alike. They were great years for me. And I am very appreciative of having the opportunity of playing with such great athletes.

God gave me a great gift and I had a lot of help developing for this occasion. Reaching this point, however, is not as important as striving to get here. This is true in all professions and all of life's activities. There are doctors, lawyers, schoolteachers, plumbers, all who strive to do their very best with their abilities.

We hear a lot today about how the American people have lost their dedication to excellence. I don't believe that is true. Each of us excels at different things, sometimes in areas that are only a hobby, more often in our life vocation. The most important thing, however, is to strive to do our very best. Nothing is more of a waste than unrealized potential. Sometimes failure to use one's talents to the fullest is the fault of the individual. Nothing could be more tragic. I am sure many of you have been to a Special Olympics and if you have, I am sure you have felt the same exhilaration I have felt in watching young people with disabilities strive as hard as they can in various events. The sense of satisfaction they get from striving is to them much more important than where they finish in the competition. As Robert Rawlings said, "A man's reach should exceed his grasp." It is striving to reach a goal that is important and if you should reach that goal, set new goals and strive for them.

A longtime basketball coach at the University of Kansas, Dr. Phog Allen, was once asked, "What was your best team?" He responded by saying, "Ask me in 25 years and let me see what they have done in life." It is not enough to rest on yesterday's triumphs, but to continually strive for new goals and accomplishments. Again, I am very deeply honored to be here today as I know the other inductees are. I hope when we look back 25 years from now, we can see this not as a zenith of our accomplishments but as a milestone in a life of striving for excellence, striving for even more distant goals.

This is a great day in the life of Gale Sayers. It is a great day for my family. It is a great day for Southern Illinois University, and I am very proud to be among the 1977 Class of Inductees. I just hope I can live up to this honor.

When I return every year to the Hall of Fame in Canton, Ohio, I enjoy visiting with former great players from my era. It is strange, though. It seems that so many of them place so much emphasis on the Hall of Fame weekend and the memories they bring back. For the most part, I am not one to live in the past and dwell on it. I like to live in the present and prepare for the future.

That has always been pretty much the way I approached my life.

After I realized I could not play football anymore, I resumed the job as a stockbroker that I had begun part time during my playing days. I also did some radio and television, which was an important step in improving my ability to communicate better.

I like to live in the present and prepare for the future. That has always been pretty much the way I approached my life.

In addition, after my retirement from football, former Dallas Cowboys coach Tom Landry asked me to become an assistant coach to work with his backfield players. I thought about that opportunity, but I could start to see the change in the attitude of many of the players back then. You know, the players who spike the ball after they score a touchdown or mug in front of the TV camera after they make a big play. That was a real turn-off for me. I told Coach Landry that I appreciated the offer, but I didn't think that job would work for me.

Back when we were playing, the players felt that the entertainment was the game on the field. Whatever you did off the field was a different story. But we wanted to entertain our fans on the field. We didn't jump up and down and turn flips and dance in the end zone. The performance was the thing for us.

Ray Lewis of the Baltimore Ravens, for example…he is a fine linebacker. But when guys like him start talking all this kind of crap…it's not going to help you win games.

When players go out of their way to do things just to be seen on camera, I don't like it.

I stayed around Chicago initially before trying my hand at athletic administration. I had already returned to the University of Kansas in 1973 to finish the requirements for my undergraduate degree and then a master's. I became athletics director at Southern Illinois University from 1976 to 1981. It was a wonderful experience and I learned a lot. It was during a time when Title IX was taking effect across the country, and issues involving fair opportunities for women in sports made it very challenging for every college administrator.

I have always been conscious of my responsibility to give back to the community and to use my celebrity as a former professional football player as a platform to help others.

At one point, I dreamed of returning to the NFL as an executive. In fact, I wrote to all 28 teams in the league at that time, asking if there might be a job available for me with my credentials. Would you believe I received just one letter back from all of those teams? It was from Al Davis, owner of the Oakland Raiders. We were unable to work out a deal, but I will never forget the fact that he was kind enough to respond to my query.

After leaving Southern Illinois University in Carbondale, I moved back to Chicago in 1981. I worked for a company called Skil Power Tools as a buyer. Then in 1983, a friend of mine named Elliott Pearlman suggested we start our own business. It was a computer business that proved to be way ahead of the times.

• • •

In 1973 I remarried, to Ardie Agee. We met at a neighborhood restaurant in Omaha, Nebraska. Ardie

After I was forced to retire from football because of injuries, I tried not to look back on my career too often. But at first it was difficult.

happened to be there to take an elderly friend to the doctor. I was at the restaurant having breakfast with my longtime friend, Vern Breakfield. Since I was going through a divorce from my first wife, Linda, I guess I was in the market for a new love in my life.

Anyway, Ardie walked past our table on her way to the cigarette machine. Vern boldly stopped her and said, "I understand you own some horses." Ardie looked startled, then said, "Yes, I do."

Vern then said, "My friend Gale here wants to buy a horse."

Ardie asked me, "What kind of a horse are you looking for?"

I started to stammer, knowing that I really had no interest in buying a horse. I just wanted to meet Ardie. But I managed to say, "Well, how many horses do you have?"

She said she had two horses, but she was not willing to sell either one.

I gave her a real sheepish look and said, "You wouldn't sell *me* one of your horses?"

After our mutual flirtation, Ardie finally asked how she would be able to get in touch with me if she did decide to sell a horse. Vern gave her his phone number. A few months went by until Vern finally told her the truth, that I wasn't really interested in buying a horse from her. I just wanted to meet her and maybe take her out.

Ardie was also going through a divorce at that time and had four sons from a previous marriage. I had three kids—two boys and a girl—from my first marriage. Ardie had grown up in the south Omaha area and, I later learned, had heard all about my football exploits. She had even previously met my mother and one of my brothers. In fact, Ardie's youngest son had played Midget Football and he wore No. 40 in honor of me.

After Ardie and I met, I asked her to watch the movie *Brian's Song* with me. I could tell that it touched her in an emotional way.

After Ardie and I got married, I went back to school at the University of Kansas and Ardie stayed in Omaha with her boys. When I got the job as assistant athletics director there, I asked Ardie to join me in Lawrence.

When I asked Ardie to marry me, she said, "First, you have to ask my boys." Her oldest son was 17 and ready to join the service. Gregory, the second oldest, was in his last year of high school, so he asked to stay with his aunt and uncle to finish high school with his friends. So it was just Ardie's two youngest boys who came with us to Lawrence. And I thought the kids adjusted pretty well. Ardie had good kids.

I have always loved children. My first wife, Linda, was having a tough time getting pregnant when we first got married, so Scott, our first son, was adopted. I had some reservations about adoption at first. But when we went to the agency and I picked Scott up, I knew right away he was ours. It just felt so right and so natural. And now Scott has grown up to be a fine young man. He is living in Columbia, South Carolina, and teaching school. He wants to become a principal. He is married and they have two daughters.

The true test of character is how you handle the stressful and sometimes tragic times.

I have been on the board of the Cradle adoption agency for 24 years. The Cradle is a private, nonprofit child welfare agency and for more than 80 years has been regarded as one of the country's foremost adoption agencies, placing 14,000 children into permanent, loving homes.

In 1994 the Cradle established the Ardythe & Gale Sayers Center for African-American Adoption. The Sayers Center is dedicated to meeting the needs of African American children, birth families, and adoptive parents.

It really bothers me to hear about people going over to Russia or other foreign countries to try to adopt children. There are so many kids right here in the United States who are desperately in need of a loving home and family.

I have always been conscious of my responsibility to give back to the community and to use my celebrity as a former professional football player as a platform to help others. In addition to being a longtime board member with the Cradle, some of my other affiliations have been as a national board member for Junior Achievement and a member of the board of trustees for Boy Scouts of America Chicago Chapter.

I have also been a board member for Marklund Children Center for handicapped children and a board member for the Better Boys Foundation. And I currently serve as president of Sayers Group LLC, a company I founded with my wife in 1984.

• • •

After I was forced to retire from football because of injuries, I tried not to look back on my career too often. But at first it was difficult. When Ardie and I would sit in front of the television to watch a football game, I would say things like, "Well, it's time for me to get taped up." And we would have a good laugh.

The early 1970s represented a challenging time of transition in my life. I saw my professional football career come to a rather abrupt end, I went through a divorce, I got remarried, and I lost my mother to cancer in 1971. And a year later, Ardie's second son was murdered.

Through all of this turmoil, Ardie told me that she was blessed to have found someone like me to make it through life's struggles. Believe me, I felt the very same way. We leaned on each other and grew as a couple. Anyone, it seems, can make it when things are going well in life. The true test of character is how you handle the stressful and sometimes tragic times.

Ardie had worked as a doctor's assistant our first year of marriage when she was in Omaha with all the kids.

But after I had asked her and two of the boys to join me at the University of Kansas, I preferred that she not work. I wanted Ardie to travel with me on the various job-related trips I had to make so we could spend more time together.

At that time of my life, it was difficult for me to meet and converse with strangers, even though I knew it was an important part of my job. Ardie was a much better conversationalist and I counted on her to carry the conversation at the many social events where I was asked to appear.

Ardie often impressed upon me the importance of communicating with people. Growing up as a youngster in Omaha, I was always very shy. I would let my athletic exploits speak for me, I guess.

I used to practice giving speeches in front of Ardie. Now I can get up and give a speech in front of hundreds of people without a hitch.

8

So Much More than Football

MY MEMORABLE STINT AS A BEARS PLAYER WAS A RELATIVE snapshot in time when I consider the span of the rest of my life. So many experiences in business, travel, education, community service, and leisure have helped define who I am and what I represent.

On August 15, 2005, for instance, I was given the rare privilege and great honor to spend 10 days visiting our military troops in Iraq and nine other countries at 18 different military bases. I was a guest of Gen. Richard Myers, former chairman of the Joint Chiefs of Staff. What I experienced was unparalleled.

I had met General Myers on a trip to San Francisco earlier that year. He had attended Kansas State University while I was a student-athlete at the University of Kansas in the early 1960s. We were staying in the same hotel in San Francisco and we swapped old stories about KU and K-State. Finally, he said, "You know, Gale, I am going to retire this year and I am going to take a 10-day trip to Iraq and visit several countries over there with the USO. Would you like to go with me!"

I thought about it for a little while, and I talked to my wife, Ardie, about it. Then I eventually decided I wanted to go. It turned out to be a life-changing event for me. General Myers and I talked to 15,000 troops during those 10 days. There were so many young people; it was unbelievable. These kids know why they are there and they know what they have to do.

Since my playing days concluded, this trip proved to be one of the most moving, eye-opening experiences I have had. When I returned from that trip, I was able to share my thoughts about that incredible experience in front of an audience during a special Veterans Day celebration that same year.

For months I had been hearing and reading the sharp criticism of every decision made by our military, and the resolution by President Bush with respect to the decision to go to war, the preparation for the war, and the lack of a plan for withdrawal.

I anticipated seeing a massive group of poorly organized, poorly equipped, poorly led, discouraged, and dispirited young men and women. That impression—promoted by debate among our politicians and projected in the media—could not have been more wrong.

What I actually saw brought a lump to my throat, warmed my heart, and made me even more proud to be an American. Our troops can be best described as a group of bright, energetic young men and women who are absolutely dedicated and enormously passionate about serving their country and protecting our way of life. They are well organized, well led, well equipped, well fed and clothed, and enthusiastic about their mission. In no way do they resemble the images often portrayed in the media and by politicians.

The trip started at Andrews Air Force Base in Maryland—the same base President Bush uses for his flights. Our first stop was Germany, where we met with army soldiers who had served a year's stint in Iraq already. A good number of them stayed in Iraq for 15 months, about three months longer than they and their families had planned. They were getting ready to go back to Iraq in a few months, and they were obviously motivated and eager to go.

What I actually saw brought a lump to my throat, warmed my heart, and made me even more proud to be an American.

From there we made stops in Kosovo, Kuwait, Iraq, an aircraft carrier in the Arabian Gulf, Korea, Japan, Alaska, and Hawaii. The aircraft did a tail-hook landing and a catapult takeoff from the aircraft carrier, which was an experience I'm happy to file away in the "been there, done that" category.

We flew on helicopters, where it was a sizzling-hot 140 degrees. It felt as if someone had a hair dryer on the highest temperature pointed right into your face. The travel and terrain were rough and rugged. Because of a damaged tire that resulted from a landing in Afghanistan, we had to get another airplane to finish the trip. It was definitely an adventure—a challenging experience, to say the least.

Everywhere we traveled, from country to country, sun up until sun down, the troops were the same—fired up and zealous about what they do for their country. General Myers's staff at the Pentagon estimated we spoke to about 15,000 troops within 10 days.

Not being sure of what I should say to all of these men and women, the general suggested I talk about the values developed and lessons learned in my career and my life. He stated that my beliefs, teachings, and wisdom go far beyond sports, and he wanted me to convey to the troops how to bring out the best in yourself and others in all areas of life. So that's what I did.

Everywhere we traveled, from country to country, sun up until sun down, the troops were the same—fired up and zealous about what they do for their country.

I stressed the importance of teamwork, because that's something football and the military service share. I was blessed with some great achievements during my football career, but I never gained a yard on my own. It took a block and a snap and a handoff for every yard I gained. It took teamwork!

Focused in our efforts, united in our goals, and connected by our collective spirit to win, that's how we won games. I think players like Terrell Owens, Kobe Bryant, Shaquille O'Neal, and a few others could stand to be reminded of that. Don't you agree?

Of course football is just a game, and what's at stake is pride and money. In sports, teamwork is a key ingredient for winning the game. But in military warfare, teamwork is essential in the face of life and death. Servicemen and servicewomen learn quickly that they must count on one another, that it is a collective effort, and that they form really close bonds because of that.

I also talked about my faith. I told them that 95 percent or more of the country was behind them. But more important, they were under the spiritual protection of a higher and greater power. I shared encouragement with persons of faith and encouraged them to never let go of their belief in the grace of our Lord and Savior, Jesus Christ. I had a number of troops come up afterward to share special scripture verses that hold particular meaning for them. Many of them shared stories about their own abiding faith and how it sustains them in the hard times.

I also told them that no matter where we are, in whatever situation we find ourselves...that it is about keeping the faith. Then it became obvious to me that these American servicemen and servicewomen are the real role models for the countries they serve, for all of us. In my message to them, I would often share a poem about being a role model:

> I'd rather see a sermon than hear one any day,
> I'd rather you would walk with me
>   than merely show the way,
> The eye's much better and more willing
>   than the ear,
> As fine words are confusing, but an example
>   is always clear,
> And the best of all the teachers are the men
>   who live their creeds,

For to see deeds in action is what
    everyone needs,
I can learn how to do it if you'll let me
    see it done.
I can watch your hands in action and see
    legs that run,
The lectures you deliver may be very wise
    and true,
But I'll get the lesson more by seeing
    what you do,
For I may misunderstand you and
    the high advice you give,
But there's no misunderstanding how you act
    and how you live.

In looking back, I'm not so certain that I inspired anyone. But there is one thing of which I am certain: they surely inspired me and left an impression that will be with me forever.

Matt Lauer from NBC's *Today Show* went with us into Iraq. He broadcast from the Baghdad Airport. No doubt the soldiers felt very good about what they were doing. If you saw the interviews that he conducted with the young soldiers, you know exactly what I mean. This wasn't an on-camera story. They were all upbeat and knew why they were there, and what they had to do.

We had a little time to sign autographs and talk to the troops one on one. We all heard the same story. And I was impressed, really, by the tremendous level of hope, devotion, and optimism from our troops. That made me think about how, in our daily routines, we find reasons to complain about physical ailments, the high prices of goods and services, our dissatisfaction with jobs. We take so much for granted, yet want so much more. We fail to acknowledge what we have because we're so concerned about what we want. We fail to give real thanks for the many blessings for which we did nothing. Blessings such as our life itself, the flowers, the trees, our family and friends...this very moment. We take these things for granted so much of the time.

Then it became obvious to me that these American servicemen and servicewomen are the real role models for the countries they serve, for all of us.

Yet here we are, safe and secure, and our lives go on as usual. In our comforts, we become numb to the recurring discussions on the war on terror and the arguments cleverly crafted by ambitious politicians and the media frenzy. All the while, the men and women in the military put themselves in harm's way—day in and day out, battling against foe and terrain in the undesirable conditions of 100- to 140-degree heat. And some military personnel are so dedicated to the cause that they are in their second and even third tours of duty in Iraq or Afghanistan.

We hear about the soldiers who die in Iraq, but we seldom hear about the many who are injured, wounded, disfigured, mangled, and defaced. Some come home with horrible injuries, mostly from improvised explosive devices. And compared to the wars of the past, our troops now have high tech body armor and good helmets. Not to mention that battlefield medical care has advanced a great deal. So what you end up with are people who survive what would have been fatal attacks 15 years ago.

We fail to acknowledge what we have because we're so concerned about what we want. We fail to give real thanks for the many blessings for which we did nothing. Blessings such as our life itself, the flowers, the trees, our family and friends...this very moment.

They survive, but they come back home with no arms, no legs, no eyes. Some even pay the ultimate price.

We visited one hospital and a soldier there had half his skull blown off. When some of the injured return home, they have no recourse but to go through tough physical therapy, and the mental battle of figuring out how to live the rest of their lives encumbered by the physical and emotional scars of the war.

Having undergone six intensive knee surgeries myself, I have some sense of the tough road they face, at least from a physical standpoint. However, I am fortunate to be able to stand on my own two legs.

Devoted to "liberty and justice for all," some injured soldiers volunteer to return to military service equipped with the aid of high-tech prostheses. Finding strength in the military honor and commitment to service, they petition to stay on the active-duty roster, ready to return to combat in the name of preserving America's cherished freedoms. These honorable men and women need our unwavering support and deserve our constant help for a long, long time.

We may think we do a lot to make the world better by expending our energies and resources through volunteer work, charitable causes, and church activities. But those in the service give so much more. They make a living by what they get, and a life by what they give. That reminds me of the adage: "Some people make things happen, and some wonder what happened."

Our soldiers continue to make things happen. They are making a life, not just a living. They make what most of us do really pale in comparison. There's a saying: "All gave some, some gave all."

But those in the service give so much more. They make a living by what they get, and a life by what they give.

Our political leaders, the media, and all the rest of us should offer a special thanksgiving for the bright, dedicated people of our military. They are brave souls who risk their own lives to protect us, to protect our country from those who seek to destroy us.

It was an honor to personally shake their hands, provide some words of encouragement, to tell them thank you for all they do, and to let them know that they make me proud to be an American.

From a personal standpoint, I recall that five of my classmates were killed in the Vietnam War. They were five people I knew very well. Those certainly were turbulent times for all of us growing up in the late '50s and '60s. The tension and pressure of war-time activity truly influenced our lives. As college students back then, we received military deforments, as long as we were in good standing academically with the university. The young men who did not attend college or flunked out of school were subject to the draft. Many kids today do not understand what that kind of pressure was like for those young men, as well as their families.

The Computer Business

I started my computer business in 1984 with a white man named Elliott Pearlman, who has been a friend of mine for 40 years. Unfortunately some people thought that I was merely fronting for my partner, lending my name to a company that I knew nothing about. Because of that, we probably missed out on some deals with the City of Chicago.

The truth is that I had to learn this computer business from the bottom up. We were doing computer servicing as well as selling supplies like ribbons, diskettes, tape, computer paper, and things like that, and I had to learn as much about that stuff as I could. It was very, very frustrating to hear people suspected I was merely using my name. But I knew that I had to learn this business and I had to get good people. I'm owner, president, and CEO of this company, but the people on the front line out there, those salespeople, they are the ones who really made my business. We are still here after 24 years, providing corporate clients Internet and security solutions; virtualization and hardware consolidation; and asset recovery solutions.

I am more proud of what I have been able to accomplish in this field than I am of what I did on the playing field. That is because football was a God-given talent. It was easy for me. But I had to learn this computer business like anybody else. People would always say, "Well, your name is Gale Sayers; you can get in the door." There is no question about that. I can get in the door. But when we went in to see customers, we came dressed to play.

When I would go to see a potential customer, it's true that I could get in a door that someone else might not get into, but I still had to come in with three things. I had to come in with good pricing, a good product, and good service. If I didn't have that, then I was just like everybody else. If I didn't deliver, people would say, "Hey, I got Gale Sayers's autograph, but his prices stink." Or they might say, "He's a nice guy, but he can't deliver a product."

Something I always tell my salespeople is to always arrive early. I say, "When we go out to see a customer, don't ever go late. If you are late, you will be fired." I have a saying: "If you are early, you are on time. If you are on time, you are late. And if you are late, you will soon be forgotten." Because we are a minority supplier, some companies think we are late all the time anyway, and I don't want to give them reason to think they are right. I always want us to be there 15 minutes ahead of time. I don't want them to wait on us; we need their business.

When we first started our business, I viewed everybody as our competition. I mean, Compaq, Hewlett-Packard...everyone. I didn't mind that. Starting out, we knew we had to go to some smaller companies for business—companies that needed to have minority credits. So we did a lot of that. But now we are at the point where we can compete with anybody: companies like IBM and Dell and Compaq. Many corporations around the country are saying that you must have a minority portion to your bid, so we can go get some of those contracts as well.

The computer business has become more competitive in the 24 years that I have been associated with it. You have more minority companies now. When we first got in the business, we were one of two minority contractors recognized: black and Hispanic. After that, there was nobody. Now there are about 12 minority contractors.

I am more proud of what I have been able to accomplish in this field than I am of what I did on the playing field.

If you come to companies like Allstate or BlueCross/BlueShield and say you are a minority contractor, you have to compete for their business like anyone else. Once again, if you don't have the pricing, product, and service, you are not getting anything. It is more difficult today for the small minority businesses because they can't compete with some of the major minority companies, and many of them are going out of business.

Starting this business was a challenge, but I never did think that we would give up on it. We felt that computers were a field of the future. We felt then that if you weren't computer literate, you would be in trouble. And that's just how it is today. Kids know that if they are not computer literate, they are in real trouble. We felt this was a field of the future and we stuck with it. We had some ups and downs, but we hung in there and we have survived.

I remember what it was like when I first started the business. Right off the bat, people would know me because of my football career, and I am glad they did. I had no problem with that. Some questioned my motives, but many of them really tried to help me. I would go see a customer and say, "I am in the computer business and I would like to get some of your business." I would send them a catalog and that type of thing to show them what we offered. The next time I would go and talk to them, they would say, "Well, Gale, we need you to get into another side of the business. Are you selling computer hardware now?"

At that point we knew it was time to get into the hardware side of the business. Nowadays, hardware sells for just 3 or 4 percent sales margins. But for our services of fixing computers, you can make 30–40 percent margins. So we have to use the service side of the business so we can make even money. Now we can do anything our customer wants us to do. We cover the whole gamut.

Even to this day, when I meet customers the first thing they want to talk to me about is football. I was in Boston on a sales trip and the first thing a customer said was, "Gale, you know I was at that 49ers game when you scored those six touchdowns." After we got done talking business, the guy said, "You know, Gale, my father was a great fan of yours. Can you sign a photograph for him?"

That is all to be expected, but we still have to deliver as a company in order to have integrity and to get the business. We understand that every time we go to see an account. And that's what I tell my employees. That's how we succeed in business.

I employ 125 people in my company now. We started our company with three people: my wife, Ardie, another young lady, and me, with Pearlman providing consultation. There were a lot of doubters at first, no question about that. Being a very small business at the beginning, we even had some doubts ourselves that it might not work. Eventually, after we started growing, we were able to get some better people. I had an old football coach a

Starting this business was a challenge, but I never did think that we would give up on it. We felt that computers were a field of the future.

long time ago who said, "There are two ways to build a winning team. Get your players better or get better players." And that is what we did in our business. We had some "players" there and we got them trained. And then we went out and got some better players. That helped us. It was tough at that time.

My first year with the computer business, I was also serving as director of athletics at Tennessee State University in Nashville for a year. I would come home on Sundays and go back on Mondays. Or sometimes I would come home to Chicago on a Saturday and check on what was going on with the computer business. That made it tough because we needed that money to live on. The computer business was not making a whole lot at that time. We also had to get a small-business loan to get started in the computer industry.

The gentleman who hired me at Tennessee State, Roy Peterson, wanted me to stay down there, but there was no way I could stay because I was trying to build our company. I told him I would give him one year. He wanted me to put in a fund-raising program and I did that for the university. But after a year I left and came back to Chicago.

My first year with the computer company, we made $30,000, and we grew from there. We got our first government contract for $150,000 in our second year of the business. It is hard getting government contracts, so that was a significant step in our development. I don't know that there was any one big deal that turned our company into a major competitor. It is just that we got better people. And Ardie got to know some people from BlueCross/BlueShield, Allstate Insurance, and International Paper. We got a lot of business from those three companies. That gave us our footing.

One thing we had to realize quickly in our business development was that we could not rely on the government set-aside programs. We had to go out and get public and private businesses. The minority set-aside programs are really tough to get and you just can't rely on them.

This company is something that we thought could happen, but I probably didn't think it would be this successful. It was through a lot of hard work. We persevered. Although I run the company and my name is on the door, I tell my people that when they come into this company, they should add their name to the title and think of ways they can make us a better company.

I have a plaque in my office with each of my employees' names that can be interchanged. The name of our company is "Sayers 40." But on my plaque I can insert each employee's name so that it says, "Jones 40" or whomever. When they come in and see that plaque, I want them to see that, hey, this is their company, too. It is not just my company; it's their company as well. So I ask them, "What can you do every day to make this a better company?" They know that I believe in that and they should be aware that they built this company. I didn't do it by myself. We are going to continue to go forward with this company. I am 64 years old. Will I retire from it? I don't know. I still enjoy what I am doing. I am not going to leave it in bad shape. I have another business partner, Jim Martin, and he has done a good job of helping me grow the company. And he may want to take it over someday. But I am going to be around several more years and continue to make it grow.

Flying Lessons

One of the more interesting things I did while I was working as the athletics director at Southern Illinois was take flying lessons. Southern Illinois is renowned for its great flying program. When I was there as director of athletics, we would fly to Chicago and St. Louis and various places to talk to alumni of SIU or other people I knew about giving us funds to support the program. We even got some money from George Halas for our program.

When I came to Southern Illinois, it was strictly a teachers' school. They didn't have any medical school or law school or anything like that. So it was tough raising money. I had to go out and work my friends because teachers didn't have any money to give us.

Anyway, one day we were flying in one of the school's planes and I asked the pilot, "What would happen if you had a heart attack or you passed out, and you are the only one who could fly this plane?"

He said, "Well, Gale, if something like that would happen, we would be in trouble."

So that's the reason I started taking flying lessons in the first place. It sounds a little silly, but that was the reason. I thought, I am up in this plane and he is the only one who can fly. Maybe if I can learn to fly the plane, should something happen to the pilot, maybe I can at least land the plane somewhere. I went through the flying program and I flew maybe 40 or 50 hours. It was enjoyable and I had great instructors.

I thought, I am up in this plane and he is the only one who can fly. Maybe if I can learn to fly the plane, should something happen to the pilot, maybe I can at least land the plane somewhere.

One day during the program I was going through what they call touch-and-gos, coming down on the runways, going around, and taking off again. To be honest, flying is easy; it's not that difficult. The problem is, if you are not instrument-rated, if you get into a cloud or something, you are in trouble. Now, I wasn't instrument-rated at the time, and while I was up there flying, I just happened to think, "I'll be damned; I'm up here all by myself. If something happens to me, it's all over." So I came in and landed and then never flew again. I guess I talked myself out of it. From that point on I decided that anytime I get on a plane, there are going to be two pilots in it.

Scuba Diving

After I left SIU and got back to Chicago, I started taking scuba-diving lessons. I enjoy scuba diving because I don't have any buoyancy in my body. When you take a deep breath, you should be able to float. I can take a deep breath, or even two deep breaths, and I go straight to the bottom. Every swimming stroke I take, I am going down.

With scuba diving, however, you are already down under the water and you have your special vest on where you can put air in it and keep you level. I enjoy that. We [Ardie and I] have been all over the world, and I have made a lot of new friends. I have a friend who still scuba dives and he is 76 years old. He dives twice a year every year. I am not into it as much as I once was because I don't think you should be doing it after a certain age, but I may go again and go down only 30 feet instead of 150 feet.

Al Tomlinson taught me a lot about diving. We have been to about 46 islands in the Caribbean, and in Australia's Great Barrier Reef and the Big Blue Hole, which is about 100 yards in circumference, in Belize. We have also fed sharks before. It is a great sport and I really enjoy it.

It is not a fast sport. You have your tanks on and you jump in. You put air into your device so you will be level when you are going through the water. It is such a great sensation. I have been down as far as 175 feet. Sport diving is 150 feet. You shouldn't dive any farther down than that. But, you know, being macho, I wanted to see a couple of things down below that. It is a great sport and there are so many things in the water. It is a whole new world. I got a camera and learned how to take pictures underwater. I have taken a lot of pictures and display them in my office for all my visitors to see.

When you are diving with a dive master, you go down with a flashlight. And as you go down, as soon as you get to 150 feet, all of a sudden it lights up. It is unbelievable. You can only stay down there about two or two and a half minutes, then you have to go back up or you could run out of air. As soon as you get back up past that 150-foot area, it is dark again. Then the dive master leads you back up there to your boat.

It is difficult to describe just how beautiful it is down there, or do it justice. You have to be there in person. It is unbelievable. In the center of the Big Blue Hole, the water is about 500 feet deep, which gives it a deep blue appearance. That's how it got its name. Just amazing!

When you are diving with a dive master, you go down with a flashlight. And as you go down, as soon as you get to 150 feet, all of a sudden it lights up. It is unbelievable.

Whereas I had some trepidation about taking flying lessons, I adapted to scuba diving pretty well. The thing about scuba diving is that you should never dive alone. You have your dive master and you have your buddy. If you dive alone, you are going to be in trouble. I never felt in danger, except for maybe one time. But you are with your dive partner and it is a very slow sport, so you should be safe under those conditions. You are kicking around down under the water, taking pictures and things like that, checking to see how much air you have got, and a compass tells you what direction you are going. It's very exciting.

Now, there is something called a drift dive that can be rather intimidating at first. A lot of times we would go to places and the water would be coming back at us. We would just relax and let the water take us and not do anything to try to resist it. The first time that happened to me, it kind of caught me off guard. In fact, I came home and wrote a poem about it. There are so many different things that you can do down there in the deep water.

There was a 2003 movie called *Open Water* that supposedly was based on a true story from 1998 about a couple that was left behind by a diving company during a session in the Great Barrier Reef in Australia. The bodies of the two American scuba-diving tourists—Tom and Eileen Lonergan—were never found in the shark-infested waters.

It's hard for me to believe that happened because they don't leave people behind. That would be awful, really. The dive master counts people to make sure everyone is together. You can't tell me that he just left those two people out there. I think that was fiction there. That would be your worst nightmare.

I don't know, but maybe you have to have a little daredevil gene in you. But I think the daredevil gene in a diver involves the question of how deep you are willing to go. I have been down far, but you can't stay down under 150 feet for more than three minutes. You have to come back up or you will run out of air. While I was in Belize I saw a wreck down there at 175 feet. I don't want to do that now, but some people want to do that all the time. Doing things like that is just foolish.

I used to dive with a fellow who weighed 360 pounds. He was a great diver and he always wanted to take chances going really deep. I would say, "See you later." But my partner and I would hang around at 100 feet or 90 feet and wait for the other guy to come back. You can get into trouble, there is no question about it. If you don't watch your air or if you are diving alone, you can get into big trouble.

I don't know, but maybe you have to have a little daredevil gene in you. But I think the daredevil gene in a diver involves the question of how deep you are willing to go.

You have to communicate with your partner and you always have to be aware, seeing what's around you. You just can't go off by yourself because you might think you're at 70 feet, and suddenly you realize that you are down to 110 feet. You have a watch on, you have a compass on, you have depth-finders on...and you need all of that stuff. But you have to always follow your dive master.

The bad part about going to these diving places is that we fly in some small planes. For example, we fly into Belize City, and then we have to take another small plane to get to the actual diving site. You see tape on the wings and other makeshift stuff like that. It's crazy. You just never know what is going to happen. But we have never had a problem on a plane or anything like that.

For the most part, I am a good flier now, even when I am traveling all over the country on business. At 6:00 in the morning, I can get on a plane and I can be asleep before the plane takes off. I have flown so much that it doesn't frighten me. The plane could be flying upside down and I would still be asleep.

I guess my favorite place to dive was the Blue Hole. It is unbelievable. It is situated about 60 or 65 miles off the mainland of Belize City. I also enjoyed the Big Barrier Reef in Australia. I saw bigger fish over there. But when I am diving, any place is fine with me. The weather is always warm and sunny. They are just beautiful places to go.

9

Omaha's Finest

MY FATHER, ROGER WINFIELD SAYERS, MADE $2,300 A year polishing cars in Omaha. I remember he had this buffer that must have weighed at least 10 pounds. After applying the paste and the wax on a car, you start the buffing process. My father always said that there is a real skill to buffing a car. If you press too hard on the car, you can buff some of the paint right off.

Regardless of what you do in life, you must always strive to be the best. And my father was considered the best car polisher around.

As a child, I remember our family moving all the time. My father might be making $55 a week on one job, then we would move to another location so he could make $5 more a week. Suffice it to say, we kids never expected to get much of anything for Christmas. My father also worked as a mechanic for Goodyear Tire and Rubber Company. And he somehow operated his own brake service out of the backyard.

My father was short—about 5′7″—but very muscular with an athletic build. He had strong biceps and long legs, relative to his short stature. He was born in Nicodemus, Kansas. He had two uncles who were the first black lawyers in western Kansas. And my great uncle, W.L. Sayers, was the state's first black county lawyer.

My father played semipro baseball as a young man. In track, he told me he once long jumped 19 feet. He also was a piano player and performed for a time with some traveling bands.

My mother must have been determined to have a girl, because the one baby picture I have seen of myself showed me with a ribbon in my hair. Oh well!

My mother, whose maiden name was Bernice Ross, was born in Gilmer, Texas, and her family moved to Wichita when she was very young. My parents somehow met and settled in Wichita.

My older brother, Roger, was born in April of 1942. My parents wanted a girl with their second child, so they had the name Gale already picked out. On May 30, 1943, I came into the world and the name Gale was pinned on me. My mother must have been determined to have a girl, because the one baby picture I have seen of myself showed me with a ribbon in my hair. Oh well!

In 1950 we moved to a little town called Speed, Kansas, in the northwestern part of the state. We moved there because my grandfather was sick and he had a big wheat farm in Speed of about 220 acres. My mother didn't want to move, but my father felt a sense of obligation. My grandfather was about 70 years old at the time.

That move began a difficult time for the Sayers family. Both of my parents began to drink heavily. My youngest brother, Ronnie, was about two years old when we moved. Roger and I, who were only 13 months apart, had to go to this tiny two-room schoolhouse. Students from grades one through six were all in one room.

As kids, we made the best of it. I remember one Christmas in particular. Our father bought us BB guns and we shot at everything in sight. That probably would not be socially acceptable to have those for young kids nowadays. One time I accidentally dropped my BB gun down a hill. I slipped trying to go after it and fell down the hill, rolling into a barbed-wire fence. It cut and scarred my back pretty severely.

After my grandfather died 16 months later, we moved to Omaha. My mother wanted to move back to Wichita, but my father's pride prevailed. My uncle, Guy Sayers, already lived in Omaha, and he offered to put us up until we found a place to live. Guy and his wife had a tiny two-bedroom house, and we all somehow managed to squeeze in there. That meant the older boys had to sleep on the floor. We were guests in that house for about two months, then we moved to the 30th Street projects.

That began a series of about nine moves in eight years. The pressure seemed to mount on my parents and they really began to drink heavily to try to escape the daily problems. We lived on Pinckney Street, moved to an apartment over a bar, then moved to 27th and Grant, then to 18th Street, then to Ohio Street, to Miami Street, and back to 30th Street.

My parents began arguing and fighting all of the time and at one point they both went to jail.

Little did I realize that our BB guns would come in handy when it came to snaring some food when we were hungry during those lean years. My brothers and I were able to shoot birds, then defeather them and cook them.

My mother did her best to feed us, but there just wasn't much to go around. We ate chicken feet a lot. She used to be able to buy 100 chicken feet for about 50 cents. My mother would either fry them or put them in a stew. The little money my father was making was going toward the $75 a month rent. And I am certain a good portion went for whisky.

I remember during my freshman year of high school, things got so bad that my mother left for about a month to stay with her cousin in Denver. Looking back now, I think she was in a state of depression. I think my mother took off like that about four times while I was growing up, but she would always return home. While she was gone, we all tried to make the best of it, and we welcomed her back warmly when she came back.

In the spring of 1970, my parents were involved in a horrible car accident. My father wound up in a coma with a fractured skull. My mother suffered some broken ribs.

Through all of the heartaches, hunger, lack of heat in the winter, and the arguing, I still loved my parents and miss them to this day. I did not realize while I was growing up that I lived in the ghetto, or the "Toe," as we later referred to it. We knew that all of our friends and acquaintances were going through the same tribulations we were going through at the time.

Perhaps the most encouraging aspect of my young life while growing up in Omaha was the opportunity to compete in sports. Whether it was football, baseball, basketball, track, or marbles, I was giving it my best shot every time. In grade school we played flag football and the backs and receivers had to wear flags or bandanas on each side of their waist. The defenders had to snatch the flags from the belt to stop the offensive player. My team won the flag football championship in the fifth, sixth, seventh, and eighth grades. And we had some players who went on to become all-city and all-state playing tackle football in high school.

My mother did her best to feed us, but there just wasn't much to go around. We ate chicken feet a lot. She used to be able to buy 100 chicken feet for about 50 cents.

Although we had to play flag football in organized grade school activities, the guys in our neighborhood were always playing tackle football in the local park. Our particular field of dreams was Kuntz Park, right in the middle of our neighborhood. It was not the most beautiful facility by any means. There were more rocks than blades of grass. But we managed to have fun and hone skills that would serve us well later in high school.

My older brother, Roger, had the same middle name as my father—Winfield—and we all called him Win. I always wanted to be as good an athlete as he was growing up. He was bigger than I was in those days, and he had tremendous speed. He actually beat former world record holder Bob Hayes in the 100-yard dash in 1962. He was, as far as I know, the only man to beat Hayes during his college career. That was quite an accomplishment.

One of my best friends was Vern Breakfield. We met in the third grade at Howard Kennedy School and remained friends after that. His father died when Vern,

> *I did not realize while I was growing up that I lived in the ghetto, or the "Toe," as we later referred to it. We knew that all of our friends and acquaintances were going through the same tribulations we were going through at the time.*

or Break, as I have always called him, was 10 years old, and their family really struggled to make ends meet. We found that we had a lot in common, including a love for music. In those days we loved to listen to Chuck Berry, Little Richard, the Platters, and all sorts of other rock 'n' roll artists. Break had all the girls around him all the time, while I was shy and awkward around them. He tried to teach me how to dance and what to say to girls at the parties. It came naturally to Break. I mainly concentrated on sports and listening to the music I loved.

Break once taught me a dance called the Run-Around. I was too bashful to ever try it on the dance floor. The dance calls for you to put one foot forward, sway from side to side, then put the other foot forward and sway from side to side.

Well, in a high school game, I was playing on defense and I intercepted a pass. Sure enough, I used the footwork from the Run-Around, eluded some tacklers, and ran 60 yards for a touchdown. I ran to the sideline so excited and I asked Break, "Did you see me use the Run-Around? Did you see me?"

Break said: "Yeah, I saw you. Man, I teach you all of these dance steps and I get you to a party and you won't even do it. You get to the game, do it, and you go 60 yards for a touchdown."

A lot of kids got in trouble growing up in our tough situation, mainly after they got involved in drinking wine or stealing things. It helped to stay involved in sports activities to keep busy and maintain a dream for a better life down the road.

We had two choices of high schools to attend on my side of town—either Tech or Central High. They were both situated in downtown Omaha. Both schools were recruiting us as athletes at the time, and I was leaning toward going to Central, since that was where my brother was going. Central's football and track coach was Frank Smagacz, and he persuaded me, Break, and our grade school fullback, Charlie Gunn, to go to Central.

Coach Smagacz was the father of 13 kids, and he still had time to work with us as athletes, students, and young men trying to find our way in life. I will be eternally grateful for what he did in terms of getting the most out of me throughout high school. His favorite saying was: "Oh you guys, you can do better than that." And, sure enough, we would try to improve on our previous effort or our previous game to do better.

Quite deservedly, Coach Smagacz was inducted in the Nebraska High School Sports Hall of Fame. He coached football and track at Omaha Central High for

27 years. His track teams won five state championships in boys track from 1958 to 1966. Smagacz was selected as the 1961 High School Football Coach of the Year in Nebraska.

We had very shoddy facilities in high school. The dirt track was one-tenth of a mile. Our distance runners had to practice in the streets. The same area where we ran track was where we practiced football in the fall. Yet we won the freshman intercity football championship with a record of 5–0–1. I played middle linebacker and halfback on my freshman team.

Break had all the girls around him all the time, while I was shy and awkward around them. He tried to teach me how to dance and what to say to girls at the parties.

By my sophomore year, I got a chance to play in the same backfield with my brother, Win. We beat Thomas Jefferson 26–0, and I gained 130 yards on seven carries and scored two touchdowns. Win also scored two touchdowns. In another game, Win scored on touchdowns of 79 and 59 yards.

As a senior, Win decided to concentrate on track and did not play football. He had won the state titles in the 100- and 220-yard dashes as a sophomore. And in his junior year he ran the 100 in 9.7 seconds and the 220 in 21.5. Since he was kind of small at 5′8″, 150 pounds, Win had been encouraged by my mother not to play football anyway. He pulled a muscle at the start of track season his senior year, however, so all the major track scholarship offers disappeared. He wound up going to nearby Omaha

University, where he excelled in track. He ran the 100 in 9.2 and the 220 in 20.5 to make the United States team that competed against Russia.

I was just very fortunate that I didn't suffer any injuries playing football in high school. I went on to lead the city in scoring in both my junior and senior years.

To this day, people ask me where and how I learned my skills as a runner. I tell them that they are God-given skills and instincts that I was blessed to have. On the football field I had tremendous peripheral vision, which allowed me to see the entire field and know when a defender was coming close or trying to tackle me. I always felt that if there was just one defender in front of me, he had no chance. Absolutely none.

At every level of football I played, there probably were other running backs who were as fast or faster than I was. But coaches used to tell me that I ran well in football gear. In other words, a lot of athletes feel uncomfortable and bogged down when they put on those shoulder pads and thigh pads. None of that bothered me one bit.

I think my experience running track in high school really helped me as a runner in football. Running the hurdles, for instance, really taught me skills to use on the football field. In my junior year I finished fourth in the state in the high hurdles.

My senior year, my biggest competition in the state long jump was Bobby Williams, a terrific all-around athlete who later played defensive back for the St. Louis Cardinals and Detroit Lions. Williams and I went back and forth with the lead in the long jump competition until our final jumps. Williams was leading with a jump of 23 feet, 3¾ inches. My best to that point was 23 feet, 2¾ inches.

On my final jump, I went 24 feet, 10½ inches—nine inches farther than the previous best high school jump in the country that year. And it was 4½ inches better than the Big Eight Conference's best jump that year. The most important part of my record leap was that it helped us win the state championship that spring. Williams was a 2001 inductee to the Nebraska High School Hall of Fame.

I will always remember some great experiences in track and field. I was on the 880-yard relay team with Vern Breakfield that won first place in 1:31.9 in 1959. My brother Win captured the state 100-yard dash title with 9.8 seconds in 1958, and the 220-yard dash in 21.7 in 1958. I won the 180-yard low hurdles in 20 seconds flat in 1961, and of course the long jump in 1961.

Win is a little more outgoing than I am. And my brother Ronnie is very much an extrovert. Ron, who was about 6′1″, 210 pounds, played football professionally with the San Diego Chargers in 1969.

My brothers never expressed any jealousy because of the success I experienced as a professional football player. For that I am very grateful. We all respect one another for what individual talents we have and what we have been able to accomplish after humble beginnings.

In fact, I am proud to join Roger in our hometown Hall of Fame of Omaha.

The Omaha Sports Hall of Fame includes interactive displays where visitors can review video highlights, photographs, artifacts, and documentation of the athletes and their careers. The Hall officially opened with a reception and ribbon cutting on May 23, 2007, followed by a special banquet highlighting each member of the 2007 class.

In addition to Roger and me, the inaugural class includes Bob Boozer, Marlin Briscoe, Connie Clausen, Eric Crouch, Bob Gibson, Nile Kinnick, Dave Rimington, and Johnny Rodgers.

Clausen encouraged the growth of women's athletics at the University of Nebraska–Omaha as a volleyball and softball coach, and she coached the 1975 national softball champions and gold medal softball team at the Pan-American Games. She has served as

> *On the football field, I had tremendous peripheral vision, which allowed me to see the entire field and know when a defender was coming close or trying to tackle me.*

chair of the Women's Softball College World Series and is a member of the NCAA Executive Committee.

Following an All-State, All-America career at Millard North High School, Crouch went on to be an All-American at the University of Nebraska, capping his senior year by winning the Heisman Trophy, the Davey O'Brien Award, and the Walter Camp Award.

An All-State football player at Omaha Benson, Kinnick went on to All-America recognition at the University of Iowa, ending his senior year with the Heisman Trophy, the Walter Camp Award, and the Maxwell Award. He was voted Male Athlete of the Year (1939) by the Associated Press, beating out Joe DiMaggio, Byron Nelson, and Joe

Lewis. Kinnick served as a pilot in the United States Navy and was killed in the line of duty during World War II on June 2, 1943.

Rimington was an All-State football center at Omaha South and a two-time All-American at the University of Nebraska. He was also winner of the Lombardi Trophy and a two-time winner of the Outland Trophy. He was named one of the 100 greatest college players of all time, and the Rimington Award, given to the nation's outstanding collegiate center, is named in his honor. Rimington is president of the Boomer Esiason Foundation.

My brothers never expressed any jealousy because of the success I experienced as a professional football player. For that I am very grateful.

I am especially proud to be in this Omaha Sports Hall of Fame with Roger Sayers.

Roger was an All-State athlete at Omaha Central and an All-American at Omaha University, a member of the 1962 United States track team, and a member of five different halls of fame.

Roger is also a two-time board president of the Urban League, two-time president of the North Branch YMCA, a 10-year campaign coordinator for the Nebraska United Negro College Fund, and a member of the board of directors of the Make-a-Wish Foundation.

Bob Gibson, another honoree, was born in Omaha in 1935 and, of course, became a Hall of Fame pitcher with the St. Louis Cardinals. Over 17 seasons with the Cardinals, he won 20 games five times and he really intimidated hitters. He was a terrific all-around athlete, and even played basketball with the Harlem Globetrotters. A lot of people don't know that he was a star basketball player at Creighton University.

The folks in Omaha are also very proud of Boozer. He is a great example of what I mean when I talk about athletes preparing themselves to quit. In 1955, Boozer averaged 25 points a game as a senior at Omaha Tech to earn All-State honors. He wound up at Kansas State and became an All-American in 1958 and 1959. Kansas State later honored him as the top vote-getter on their 10-man Team of the Century.

Boozer won a gold medal with the 1960 Olympic team. He was the first player taken in the 1959 NBA draft and played 11 years with the Chicago Bulls, Seattle Supersonics, Milwaukee Bucks, Cincinnati Royals, New York Knicks, and Los Angeles Lakers. He made the NBA All-Star team in 1968 and won an NBA title with the Bucks in 1971.

When his playing days were over, Boozer completed an Olympic torch run through Omaha by lighting a cauldron that was part of a downtown ceremony.

Boozer spent 27 years working at Northwestern Bell, which became U.S. West. The last 10 of those years were as a federal lobbyist. He retired in 1997 and soon after was selected to serve on the Nebraska Board of Parole.

Yet another Omaha product who came along after I did, Johnny "the Jet" Rodgers was voted High School Athlete of the Year.

At the University of Nebraska, Rodgers served as a punt return specialist, pass receiver, and running back.

He wound up breaking almost all of the records for the Cornhuskers and was a two-time All-American. He earned both the Walter Camp Award and the Heisman Trophy in 1972, and was later voted University of Nebraska's Player of the Century.

Rodgers was a first-round draft pick of the San Diego Chargers, but he signed a huge contract to play in Montreal for the Montreal Alouettes of the Canadian Football League. A real fan favorite in Canada, Rodgers won the CFL's Most Outstanding Rookie award in 1973. He played four years in Canada and helped lead his team to the Grey Cup championship in 1974. He returned to the United States in 1977 to sign with the Chargers. Injuries to his leg and knee ended his career in the NFL.

Rodgers was inducted into the College Football Hall of Fame and was voted the Most Valuable Player in the history of the Big Eight Conference. Today, Rodgers is a businessman in Omaha, where he operates a sports marketing company and bedding products manufacturer. He also works with his alma mater to encourage athletes who dropped out of school to return and complete their education.

Marlin Briscoe was the first black starting quarterback in pro football in 1968 for the Denver Broncos, who were then in the American Football League. Before being drafted in 1968, Briscoe played football at Omaha South High School and at the University of Omaha. The Denver Broncos were pretty much forced to start Briscoe in 1968 after their first- and second-string quarterbacks got hurt early in the season. Briscoe came in and played the final

11 games and threw a team rookie record 14 touchdown passes.

Still, the Broncos would not let Briscoe compete for the starting job the next year and wound up trading him to Buffalo, where he launched a brilliant career as a wide receiver. In 1970, Briscoe became an All-Pro receiver for the Bills. From 1972 to 1974 he played for the Miami Dolphins and won two Super Bowl rings. He ended his pro career in 1976 with New England.

"They are not looked at as black quarterbacks now. They are looked at as quarterbacks," Briscoe said. "They get booed if they don't play well."

I appreciated what Briscoe had to say in the *Chicago Tribune* when he was asked recently what he thought of the plethora of black quarterbacks in the NFL today. "They are not looked at as black quarterbacks now. They are looked at as quarterbacks," Briscoe said. "They get booed if they don't play well. We've gone past what color they are. It hasn't always been that way. In 1969, the year after my debut with Denver, one of my proudest moments was the fact that four African American quarterbacks were drafted. And that never would have happened if I hadn't been successful."

Briscoe maintains his awareness of the changes in the NFL over the decades. "There had to be a black quarterback before they had a black coach," he said. "The progression was to show that on the world stage a black man could lead on the field at that level. Then we saw what Doug Williams could do in the Super Bowl to give credence to the abilities of the black man in that position. And then, of course, there was Warren Moon getting inducted [as the first black quarterback in the Hall of Fame]. Getting black coaches was the next level to break into. Then the areas for advancement include getting more black executives and, hopefully, black ownership."

On the same day in 1968 that Briscoe became the first black starting quarterback in the NFL, his teammate, Walter Highsmith, became the first black starting center in a game against the Cincinnati Bengals. "That kind of went under the radar," said Briscoe.

Briscoe feels there were several potentially capable black coaches who could have succeeded in the NFL in the 1960s and '70s, had they been given an opportunity. "Guys like Pete Richardson, Eric Crabtree, and Larry Little come to mind. Very smart individuals," said Briscoe, who also briefly assisted Chuck Fairbanks at the University of Colorado following his playing days.

"What is happening today just gives credence to the notion that a person could succeed if given the opportunity," he said as the Steelers announced the hiring of Mike Tomlin to become their next head coach.

Josh Gibson was a great baseball player in the 1930s and '40s in the Negro Leagues. I was told that he played in Latin America during the winter months and some summers as well. I have heard so many horror stories about how blacks were treated in those days, even outstanding ballplayers such as Josh Gibson.

Gibson was known as "the Babe Ruth of the Negro Leagues." He played 17 years for the Pittsburgh Crawfords and the Homestead Grays. Word was, he hit 84 home runs one season and may have had as many as 800 runs in his career. He is said to be the only man to have hit a fair ball out of New York's Yankee Stadium. He was elected to the Baseball Hall of Fame in 1972.

Ahman Green of the Houston Texans is probably the most prominent athlete from Omaha who is still active. Green is a product of my old high school—Omaha Central. He was a high school All-America selection and state Player of the Year.

Green also was a two-time academic All-State selection in high school, and he later earned Academic All–Big 12 honorable mention in 1990 at Nebraska.

Between the 2000 and 2004 NFL seasons, Green rushed for more yards and gained more total yards from scrimmage than any other running back in the NFL while with the Green Bay Packers.

During his collegiate career Green compiled 3,880 rushing yards and 42 touchdowns, both totals good for second place on the Cornhuskers' all-time list. He also posted 300 yards and three touchdowns on 35 catches.

Omaha Central High School is now the oldest high school in Nebraska. It is located at 124 North 20th Street in downtown Omaha. Its current enrollment is about 2,500 students, and it has a traditional college preparatory curriculum, as well as honors and advanced placement programs. The student body has always been diverse, and now includes international students from all over.

Omaha Central has produced more than famous athletes. Two Nobel Prize winners have come out of my alma mater, as well as the inventor of Rogaine, Dr. Guinter Kahn; former Nebraska senator Edward Zorinsky; the producer of the TV show *Primetime Live*, Howard Rosenberg; and American philosopher Saul A. Kripke. I am also proud to say that famous actor Henry Fonda lived in Omaha.

So you see, Omaha Central is known for much more than the great athletes it has produced. I am grateful for the academic foundation my high school provided me.

10

Those Elusive Championships

JUST LIKE ANY OTHER DIEHARD CHICAGO BEARS FAN, I watched the team's 2006 season with particularly keen interest.

At the start of the season, few people predicted they would wind up as National Football Conference champions, competing in the Super Bowl for the first time in 21 years. But as the season progressed, it became clear that the NFC was theirs for the taking. In fact, the Bears' NFC North Division lacked any clear-cut competitor because the Packers, Lions, and Vikings played very inconsistently.

Yet it also became clear to me early on that young Rex Grossman was not the quarterback capable of winning a Super Bowl for the Bears. Not in the 2006–07 season, anyway. It always has been my contention that there should be competition at every position from training camp throughout the regular season. These are high-paid professionals we are talking about, and competition only makes athletes better. The Bears seemed to coddle and protect Grossman, for whatever reason, and I believe that hurt him and the team in the long run.

Bears general manager Jerry Angelo signed veteran Brian Griese as a backup quarterback during the off-

The Bears seemed to coddle and protect Grossman, for whatever reason, and I believe that hurt him and the team in the long run.

season, but coach Lovie Smith decided not to give him significant playing time, even when Grossman struggled miserably at times—turning the ball over numerous times with fumbles and interceptions, several of which were returned for touchdowns.

Why not give Griese a shot and see what he can do? I don't understand that strategy at all. Grossman was clearly inexperienced and inconsistent, but that particular Bears team was prepared to win it all in the 2006 season if the quarterback position had been more solid.

I hope the Bears are able to come back from their 29–17 Super Bowl XLI loss to Indianapolis. The Bears were 13–3 during the 2006 regular season, but there are no guarantees they will be back in the Super Bowl right away. That is the nature of the NFL these days. There are no true dynasties. The NFL owners wanted parity in the league, and that is what they have gotten. Every year, it seems, a team that had a losing record the year before emerges with a playoff bid the very next year. Look at the New Orleans Saints. They were 3–13 in 2005 and nearly made it to the Super Bowl the next season behind first-year head coach Sean Payton.

A lot of the current Bears impressed me with their performances in 2006. Everyone asks me about the rookie kick returner Devin Hester. No question, he is a special athlete who should have a brilliant future. Heck, he already set the NFL record with six kick returns for touchdowns during the regular season. Then he startled everyone with a 92-yard kickoff return for a TD to start Super Bowl XLI.

I don't know what else he could do to prove himself, except to maintain that kind of explosiveness and stay healthy throughout his career. I know there was a lot of debate over whether Hester should be used on offense, since he proves so elusive as a kick returner and made the NFC Pro Bowl team. I think the Bears tried him a couple of times as a wide receiver toward the end of the season, but he never broke a big play from scrimmage.

Speaking from experience, I know that it is more difficult to find an open space to run when you start from the line of scrimmage as a receiver.

Speaking from experience, I know that it is more difficult to find an open space to run when you start from the line of scrimmage as a receiver. Hester is not that big, and perhaps not as physical as some receivers, so it is harder for him to get off the line. He played some cornerback and nickel back, as he did in college at the University of Miami, so I don't know what the Bears' plans might be to get the ball in his hands more. He certainly is an exciting player and very deserving of his recognition after his first season in the NFL.

So much credit has to go to Smith and GM Angelo. They won their division in 2005 and then the NFC title in 2006. It's great and everyone should be proud of the Bears organization.

They already have made some significant off-season decisions by not re-signing defensive coordinator Ron Rivera, replacing him with assistant coach Bob Babich, and placing a franchise tag on outstanding linebacker Lance Briggs. After a seemingly drawn-out negotiation, Smith had his contract renewed on March 1, 2007, for an additional four years and a $22 million package. That puts Smith in the top third of NFL coaching salaries, which is where his record should place him.

Any athlete in any sport will tell you they want to play for the championship. Sure, the individual records are nice, but a team championship is the true coronation of an athlete's career.

I was not fortunate enough to play on a championship team during my brief career with the Bears. Even though we had several future Hall of Fame players on those rosters, we were never able to get all of the stars aligned to win it all. I really wish I had had a chance to play in a Super Bowl. Any athlete in any sport will tell you they want to play for the championship. Sure, the individual records are nice, but a team championship is the true coronation of an athlete's career.

Over the years that I played, we had Mike Ditka, Dick Butkus, Doug Atkins, Bill George, Stan Jones, and myself—all Hall of Fame players. But it just goes to show you that football is the ultimate team sport. It takes outstanding contributions from every phase of your teams—offense, defense, and special teams—to win it all.

Some of the Hall of Fame players on those teams I played on were toward the end of their careers by the time I got there. It seemed like so many of the veterans got old overnight. Ditka was traded to Philadelphia in 1967; Jones finished his career in Washington in 1966; Atkins would wind up in New Orleans; and George retired right after I arrived.

11

Land of Opportunity

I HAVE WITNESSED MANY RACIAL INJUSTICES OVER MY lifetime. I certainly did not take lightly the social significance of having two black men coaching in the Super Bowl in 2007 for the first time ever.

Lovie Smith took his Bears into Miami for Super Bowl XLI against the Indianapolis Colts' Tony Dungy. But what took so long? We are finally making some long-overdue progress in that area. There were no black coaches in the NFL when I played. Now you have Herm Edwards in Kansas City, Marvin Lewis in Cincinnati, Mike Tomlin with the Pittsburgh Steelers, Romeo Crennel with the Cleveland Browns, and Smith and Dungy.

When Dennis Green was fired in Arizona and Art Shell was bounced in Oakland, the reason clearly was that they did not win enough games. The fact that they are black was not the issue, which is the way it should be.

We have been through so much in our society when it comes to breaking barriers. When I was playing, the big issue was giving black quarterbacks an opportunity to play and start in the NFL. Now there are so many black quarterbacks that it is hardly a topic of conversation.

That is not to say there aren't inequities in the coaching and management landscape in the NFL, especially

That is not to say there aren't inequities in the coaching and management landscape in the NFL, especially when you consider that 67 percent of the players in the league today are African American.

when you consider that 67 percent of the players in the league today are African American.

No doubt it took pressure applied to NFL owners from equal rights groups before many of them even bothered to interview a minority head coaching candidate. Thanks to the "Rooney Rule" introduced by the venerable owner of the Pittsburgh Steelers, all teams are required to at least interview a minority candidate when an opening develops.

Several years ago, an executive committee was formed to analyze the plight of African American head coaches and head coaching candidates in the NFL. At that time, there were just two black coaches in the NFL—Dungy and Edwards, then with the New York Jets.

The committee, which included the late attorney Johnnie Cochran and Cyrus Mehri, applied methods of statistical analysis similar to those developed in civil rights enforcement cases at major corporations such as Texaco, Coca-Cola, Johnson & Johnson, and Bell South.

"Wins and losses—the currency of football and all team sports—form the statistical heart of this report," the committee members wrote.

A database was created that includes the win-loss records of each head coach in the NFL over the past 15 years.

Labor economist Dr. Janice Madden of the University of Pennsylvania compared the overall performance of the five African American head coaches at that time—Shell, Green, Ray, Rhodes, and Dungy—with all the other head coaches during this period.

Madden determined that:

- The black coaches averaged 1.1 more wins per season than the white coaches.

- The black coaches led their teams to the playoffs 67 percent of the time versus 39 percent of the time for the white coaches.

- In their first season, black coaches averaged 2.7 more wins than the white coaches in their first season.

- In their final season, terminated black coaches won an average of 1.3 more games than terminated white coaches.

- The black coaches inherited teams with an average of 7.4 wins per season and, during their tenures, increased the average wins for their teams to 9.1 per season.

Critics of this study asserted the statistical pool is too small to draw widespread conclusions. But whose fault is it that the pool of black coaches is so small? And if these statistics are correct, why should black coaches be held to a higher standard than white coaches?

I say, let's allow every qualified candidate into the pool.

The college enrollment of minority students has increased 57 percent nationwide since the 1980s. But those percentages are not reflected in the most visible athletic leadership positions across the country.

John Thompson, the former longtime Georgetown University basketball coach, has a practical perspective on the plight of black assistants seeking head coaching positions in college football and basketball.

"Unfortunately, in our society we still have a lot of people who, because they do not socialize with or go to church with or operate in business with a lot of minorities, they are not comfortable enough to make decisions that relate to minorities progressing in society," Thompson told the *Chicago Tribune*. "I think the Black Coaches Association sometimes can bridge that gap, or organizations like the BCA, to help create that comfort level.

"In a lot of areas there has been change, but by the same token, I think there is a need for more," Thompson continued. "There is a responsibility on our side too, to put ourselves in a position where we can take advantage of those opportunities. People don't prepare themselves for things they know they do not have a chance to participate in. It is interesting for [employers] to run around and say they can't find a lot of qualified [minorities]. When I see a black person as a writer, I know that there is a possibility of a student that I have becoming a writer. But if I never see you as a writer, then there is no need for me to prepare that student to become a writer."

I say, let's allow every qualified candidate into the pool.

Thompson always has been outspoken in his views about racial inequality in sports and society. Other successful minority coaches, including Colts boss Tony Dungy, have taken a more subtle approach.

"There is room for more than one way of getting things accomplished. That is my personality," said Dungy, who toiled silently for years as a highly qualified assistant before receiving a chance to become a head coach in the NFL.

"I think people should follow their heart," added Thompson. "We should also realize that we are not just representing ourselves. Unfortunately, in this society, so many people reflect on your ability to do something based on what they see another minority, another black do. And that's just the reality of it. We have to be careful in some instances with that."

An NCAA study shows that among athletics directors, who are primarily responsible for hiring coaches, the number of blacks dropped to less than 3 percent at major colleges in 2001, down from 4 percent in 1995.

Growing up in Omaha, I didn't seem to experience many overt signs of racism, mainly because I spent most of my time in the all-black area of town. I had very few white associates, even though my high school had only about 50 black guys in the school out of about 1,500 students. We had seven black starters on the football team. Oh, sure, there were isolated incidents in which we heard the "N" word used, but it seems as though those memories have been repressed in our minds over the years. It wasn't until my senior year of high school that I encountered what I felt was a blatant racist slight.

The *Omaha World Herald* newspaper would always choose its Athlete of the Year in the state of Nebraska. Well, my senior season was the year that I had set the city scoring record in football. I had been selected for the high school All-America team and the All-Midwest team. Dick Butkus also had been selected for that honor squad. In addition to that, I had won three gold medals in the state track meet as a senior, including a state record in the long jump.

Yet I wasn't picked as Athlete of the Year.

The newspaper decided to pick a young man named Kent McCloughan from Broken Bow, Nebraska. Now, McCloughan was a fine athlete and he went on to become a defensive back with the Oakland Raiders. But in high school he came from a smaller, Class B school where he was a running back. He also won two medals in the state track meet. They called him the Custer County Comet because he won the 220-yard dash and tied for first in the 100.

He was an exceptional athlete, but I still felt I was better and from a larger city with tougher competition. I have never been one to constantly play the race card, but I was convinced the only reason I did not receive that honor was that he is white and I am black.

As fate would have it, I faced McCloughan in the state's annual East-West Shrine Game. The game featured the top players in the state, divided into the North and South teams. McCloughan wound up on the North squad and I was on the South.

I have never been one to constantly play the race card, but I was convinced the only reason I did not receive that honor was that he is white and I am black.

We clobbered the North team 32–0. I also played middle linebacker on defense in that game and I had a chance to tackle McCloughan very hard. I slammed him to the ground in the third period and he ended up sitting out the rest of the game. I managed to score four touchdowns on offense, catching TD passes of 51 and 26 yards and running for scores from 43 and 27 yards out. I was really keyed up for this encounter and it gave me great pleasure to do well and try to prove any critics I had wrong. I now realize that McCloughan had nothing to do with the selection committee but at the time it was good to take my anger out on an opponent.

I was voted the game's Most Valuable Player. That made me feel a lot better about not being named Nebraska Athlete of the Year, and my parents were in the stands to watch me.

After my senior year of football, I received 100 college scholarship offers. I remember visiting seven schools— Iowa, Iowa State, Northwestern, Notre Dame, Minnesota,

Nebraska, and Kansas. My friend and teammate, Vern Breakfield, went with me on most of the trips.

I ended up signing 17 letters of intent, indicating that I would enroll in their university. I was young and naïve and just having a great time enjoying all of the trips.

After visiting Iowa State first and signing a letter of intent, an article turned up in the paper that I was headed there to play for head coach Clay Stapleton.

Then I visited Iowa and I was excited about their program because of their razzle-dazzle offense. But their head coach at the time, Jerry Burns, spent so much time trying to entice Henry Carr to become a Hawkeye that he didn't spend any time with me. Carr, a sprinter who won a gold medal in the 200 meters in the 1964 Olympics, was a running back in high school and he wound up going to Arizona State.

I had a great time visiting Notre Dame in South Bend, Indiana. I had just flown for the first time in my life when I visited Northwestern. Then Break came with me for his first flight ever to go to Notre Dame.

It was snowing and we were both kind of nervous, but we tried to act cool. The plane had to stop in Cedar Rapids, Iowa, and it was shaking kind of funny. The plane ended up sliding past the runway by 150 feet or so. Break took a quick trip to the bathroom and I felt fixated, just sitting there in my seat. The pilot got the plane up and going again and we made it to South Bend.

We met Notre Dame coach Joe Kuharich there. And Jim Snowden, who later played for the Washington Redskins, showed me around the campus. Break and I got to see a

Notre Dame basketball game and Break threw some popcorn out on the court after a controversial call. The refs gave Notre Dame a technical foul.

We got back to the dorm before the 10:00 PM curfew, but we still had time for some mischief. Break and I put crackers in all the other guys' beds. After they took showers and got into bed, you could hear all of the crackling throughout the dormitory. Later on that night we continued doing stupid stuff like running up and down the halls and knocking on doors before disappearing. One time I was running down the hall with my shorts on and Break locked the door to our room, leaving me in the hallway.

A student priest walked down the hall and I had to hide behind a corner. When Break finally let me in the room, we wrestled for an hour because I was so mad. But actually we had a blast.

I finally decided against Notre Dame because I felt it was too far from home.

That left Nebraska as a strong possibility, since it was just 60 miles from Omaha. Even Omaha University got into the bidding for me. That's where my brother Win went, and he did quite well on the track team. And my younger brother, Ronnie, also went to Omaha and he got drafted by the San Diego Chargers in 1969.

But Nebraska recruited me pretty strong. An alumnus from Nebraska gave me a job after football season my senior year of high school. I would wash a couple of cars and he would give me $25. Then another alumnus bought me a stereo and clothes and gave me the use of a car.

Nebraska promised my father pretty much anything he wanted if I went there. There was a lot of pressure on everybody. But I was not all that pleased with the way I was treated on my visit to Nebraska.

I guess Break and I broke one of the cardinal rules of young high school recruits. We wore our high school letter sweaters on campus. We thought they were sharp, with all the stars showing our achievements in football and track.

> *I guess Break and I broke one of the cardinal rules of young high school recruits. We wore our high school letter sweaters on campus.*

But the Nebraska officials didn't like that. They wanted all of the recruits to pretty much dress alike. We wore the sweaters everywhere we went anyway. So one of Nebraska's top running backs, Willie Ross, saw us with our letter sweaters. He was ready to jump us and rough us up. He started hollering at us and making a commotion. Ross's teammate, another Nebraska back named Thunder Thornton, kept holding Ross back. We yelled, "Let him go; we'll get him." We didn't end up fighting, but it really soured our experience that weekend.

To add to that episode, the Nebraska officials ended up putting me and Break in the dormitory basement where they had heating pipes along the ceiling. The pipes kept making noise and Break said: "I wouldn't come down to this college if they gave us a million dollars, man. They came down to recruit us and they put us in a room like that."

Plus, we found out later that four high school recruits from Oklahoma had been housed in nice rooms upstairs.

We stayed for a dance at the student union and found out there were 44 black athletes at Nebraska and only two black girls. When the word got out that we didn't enjoy our visit to Nebraska, the head football coach, Bill Jennings, came to Omaha and took us out for a nice dinner. We were at a fancy restaurant, the type I was not accustomed to frequenting. I was trying to cut my steak and it flew off the table.

I ended up taking a pass on Nebraska as Jack Mitchell began recruiting me for Kansas. Mitchell was full of a lot of talk, but he was a dynamic personality and he got my attention. His top recruiter was assistant coach Tom Triplett, who had seen me play several times.

During the visit to Kansas, I fell in love with the campus right away. I got to meet basketball star Bill Bridges and star halfback Curtis McClinton, who showed me around and told me how great it was at KU. There were two black fraternities and two black sororities on campus.

I loved the fact that Kansas was a top football team in the Big Eight at that time. The only issue was that it was 180 miles from home, but I could deal with that.

I had made up my mind to go to Kansas, which really irritated the people in my home state who figured I should go to Nebraska. I received hundreds of angry phone calls and letters. And the letters continued all through school at Kansas. But I was certain I had made the right choice for me.

I enjoyed a very productive three-year varsity career under Coach Mitchell at Kansas in the early 1960s. I was able to set Big Eight records by rushing for 2,675 yards, catching passes for 408 yards, and adding 835 yards on kick returns.

On November 28, 1957, Mitchell, then 33, had been named Kansas University's 30th head football coach following the departure of Chuck Mather, who, under pressure, tendered his season's-end resignation with four games left on the '57 schedule. Mitchell came from the University of Arkansas, where he led the football program for three seasons.

Mitchell would coach the Jayhawks for nine seasons. In December of 1966—two years after I had left the program—he agreed to a buyout of a 10-year contract extension that would have run through the 1970 season. The agreement was reached following 2–8 and 2–7–1 seasons. Mitchell posted a cumulative 44–42–5 record while at Kansas. His total head coaching record at Wichita, Arkansas, and KU was 74–59–7.

When Mitchell took the job in 1957, he was given a five-year deal that paid him $15,000 a year. I guess that seemed like a lot of money back then. Mitchell, who had been the Arkansas coach since 1955, had been considered a top prospect for the job since before Mather resigned.

Dr. Franklin Murphy proudly announced at that initial press conference: "Fifteen thousand dollars is *the* compensation. I have read of a number of fringe benefits, such as TV and radio commitments, and others, but there are none of those in this commitment. Mr. Mitchell is the choice of the director of athletics, A.C. Lonborg."

Although the salaries of major college football coaches today dwarf what they made back in the 1950s and '60s, the measuring stick of wins and losses has always been pretty much the same. On December 5, 1966, the positive tone during the hiring of Coach Mitchell in 1957 had been replaced with the somber atmosphere of a firing.

Kansas began its search for a new football coach after the Athletic Board and Mitchell reached a "mutually satisfactory" agreement. Mitchell was to be paid $14,000 a year, for a total of $56,000 for the final four years of his contract. That was about 70 percent of what would constitute full payment. He would be paid through June 30, 1967, at his then $20,300 a year salary.

Mitchell's successor was 35-year-old Franklin C. "Pepper" Rogers, who came to Kansas after a stint as backfield coach at UCLA. Rogers signed to a four-year deal, and after four seasons and a 20–22 record—which included

I had made up my mind to go to Kansas, which really irritated the people in my home state who figured I should go to Nebraska. I received hundreds of angry phone calls and letters.

a terrific 1968 season that culminated in a trip to the 1969 Orange Bowl—he was offered a chance to return to UCLA as head coach.

A tearful Rogers announced his resignation at Allen Fieldhouse on January 8, 1971. Pepper expressed his reluctance to leave the KU fans but said he had confidence in incoming coach Don Fambrough.

On April 24, 1998, I was pleased to be honored by my alma mater with the Apple Award for Distinguished Achievement in Education at KU. One of the speakers was Coach Mitchell. Since 1994, I had helped the school raise more than $45,000 for student scholarships through the Gale Sayers Benefit Golf Tournament.

The award recognizes KU education alumni "who have demonstrated through their achievements the qualities of professionalism and those personal characteristics which reflect the mentoring spirit to inspire students" and who are "currently active in education and civic organizations which strive for the high ideals of the profession and to promote these ideals in public."

Other speakers at the event included Dave Schmidt, National Advisory Board chair; Bob Frederick, KU athletics director; Wayne Osness, KU professor of health, sport, and exercise science and my student teaching adviser; and Clay Blair III, past chair of the National Advisory Board.

In addition to assisting my alma mater with fundraisers, I continue to make cancer research a lifetime priority. I had two very special people pass away with that dreadful disease: my mother died of ovarian cancer and, of course, Brian Piccolo died of embryonal-cell carcinoma. It will always be a priority in my life.

12

Show Me the Money!

I NEVER HAVE BEEN ONE TO LIVE WITH REGRETS ABOUT the past, and I thoroughly enjoyed playing professional football in the era that I played. But it is interesting to see how the game has evolved, how soaring television revenue has helped make multimillionaires out of some fairly average NFL players today. God bless them. And I realize that the window of financial opportunity is small, considering that the average NFL career is just about three and a half years.

So many players today say their decisions are not based on the money. But look at the Bears' Lance Briggs and his threat to sit out the 2007 season if the Bears didn't trade him or sign him to a rich long-term contract. The Bears put the franchise tag on him, meaning they would retain the rights to him by paying him a guaranteed $7.2 million. He is getting the average of the top five players at his position. That means he is regarded as one of the top players in the game.

Briggs finally agreed to stay with the Bears by signing a one-year, $7.2-million contract at the start of training camp. When I played, it used to be about winning championships, but now it is only about the money, because there is so much out there. But how much does it take for you to live? It is amazing what these players are making.

We laid the foundation and put that road up there so the players today could come in and get that money.

The players are so different today and I just wish they knew the history of the game. Today they say that the money comes from CBS, NBC, ABC, FOX Sports, and ESPN. But if the players weren't good back then at the beginning of pro football, then television would not have come up with the money to pay the players so much today. We laid the foundation and put that road up there so the players today could come in and get that money. If we had had bad players and bad teams back in those days, the league wouldn't be what it is today.

Nowadays, college football players are permitted to leave school early and join the NFL. I did not have that option when I was playing at Kansas, and to be honest, the big money wasn't there in the NFL back then to make it a worthwhile possibility. I am glad I stayed at Kansas and earned most of my credits for graduation before going to the Bears. I went back to Kansas later to pick up my undergraduate and master's degrees.

When I look at the young star athletes today who are offered the opportunity to go into pro football or basketball, I honestly cannot fault them for taking the chance. When the money is that big and you are talking about getting a $10 million or $15 million signing bonus, how could you blame anybody for taking that? With that kind of money up front, even if you got hurt you could live the rest of your life on Easy Street.

I hope that one day those athletes who leave school early to take the big professional sports money will go back and finish their education. They probably one day will get married and have kids. Will their kids grow up and become professional athletes? Probably not. So they are going to need something to fall back on.

I also hope that these young professional athletes get themselves a financial adviser, because if they don't, it is easy to imagine them losing it all with some bad choices. There are a lot of pressures, especially on athletes who come from poor backgrounds. They are expected to buy their parents a new house or a new car or to take them on exotic vacations. Then the athlete might have his own new cars and his own three houses, and all of a sudden the money is gone. Then you have nothing.

Here is an example of how times have changed in the National Football League. Today the members of the winning Pro Bowl team receive $25,000 apiece, and the losing team gets $20,000 each. Even with that incentive, it seems like half of the Pro Bowl players today always try to get out of going over to Hawaii to play in that game. They will make up excuses and say that they hurt their little finger or their foot is sore. It's amazing.

I played in four Pro Bowls and was named the game's MVP three times. I used to look at that Pro Bowl game as our Super Bowl back then. It was a chance to prove to people that I was the best.

Guess how much we were paid for those games? The winners got $1,000 apiece and the losers received $500 each. But when we played in that game, it was a big deal. Players like Deacon Jones and others would fight like dogs for that money. We didn't play the Pro Bowl in Hawaii back then. It was always in Los Angeles. It is so sad that these players today don't appreciate it. I guess it is all about the money again. The $25,000 that the Pro Bowl winners make today...that was the same amount I signed for when I first started playing with the Bears in 1965.

The $35,000 that the Pro Bowl winners make today... that was more than my entire yearly salary when I first started playing with the Bears in 1965.

There weren't a lot of endorsement opportunities back then either, especially for black athletes. I had a deal with Wilson Sporting Goods and Carnation Milk. That was about it. You rarely saw another black face out there endorsing products until Muhammad Ali.

I was always preparing to quit, as I like to say. Right after the 1967 season, for instance, I took a 10-week course at the New York Institute of Finance to study for my stockbroker's license. My teammate at the time, halfback Jon Arnett, was the first one to talk to me about studying to become a stockbroker. He had experienced success himself in that field in Los Angeles. I even sought advice on that subject from Coach Halas, and he sent me around to several places in Chicago to get a sense of what that business is all about.

I remember taking 20 tests during that 10-week course, plus a final exam. It wasn't easy by any means. And I even had to miss one week of the class when I played in the Pro Bowl that January. When I returned for the class, I was given a tutor to help me make up for the week I missed. I took the final exam a week after everyone else in my class. It was on a Friday. I was nervous all weekend, thinking I had passed it but not being certain. By Monday I found out I had passed the test. And later I would become the first black stockbroker for Paine, Webber's Chicago office.

• • •

How much money could I command if I were playing in the NFL today?

That is a hypothetical question, so let's consider a hypothetical answer. I simply would say that if I did the same things on the football field that I did back then, I think it would be fair to say I should be paid in the range of the top quarterbacks today. After all, the quarterbacks are the highest-paid players in the league.

My NFL statistical totals included 9,435 combined net yards, 4,956 yards rushing, and 336 points scored in just seven seasons. I am the NFL's all-time leader in kickoff return average. I won All-NFL honors five straight years and was named Offensive Player of the Game in three of the four Pro Bowls in which I played.

I think the fact that I excelled as both a running back and kick returner made me such a valuable weapon. And I really enjoyed catching passes out of the backfield. If you got me the ball in an open space with just one or two defenders in front of me, I generally won that battle easily.

The kick returns gave me an opportunity to touch the ball many more times. The Bears wanted me back there returning kicks and I wanted to be there. I was never frightened, even though I knew there were 11 defenders running full speed toward me, ready to rip my head off.

I was blessed with great peripheral vision, which allowed me to see the entire field. I returned kicks in high school and college, as well. So it did not faze me one bit to do that in the NFL. I never got hit solidly on a punt return or kickoff return.

When it came to running the football from scrimmage, most of the Bears offensive linemen knew that all they had to do was get in the way of somebody and I could find daylight. Mike Pyle, George Seals, Bob Wetoska, Mike Rabold…those offensive linemen always did enough for me to break into the open, and I very much appreciated the work they did.

My frame of thinking was always to prepare for the unexpected. What if they missed a block? That is what went through my mind. With my peripheral vision I would be looking at ways to avoid a direct hit in that case. No one had ever taught me anything about running the football. Maybe a coach had reminded me about changing hands with the football to make sure it was on the outside toward the sideline in case of a fumble. But other than that, everything pretty much came naturally to me.

I have never been a selfish player and the individual stats don't mean nearly as much to me since we were unable to win a title during my career. But there are times when I wonder how much more effective I could have been as a running back if we had been fortunate enough to have a steady, more reliable quarterback situation during my career.

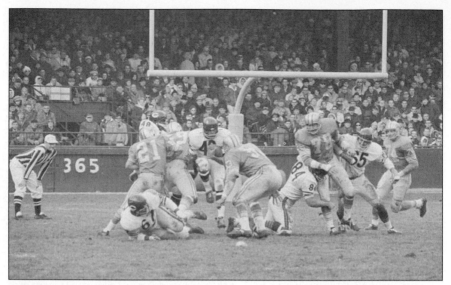

I think the fact that I excelled as both a running back and kick returner made me such a valuable weapon. And I really enjoyed catching passes out of the backfield. If you got me the ball in an open space with just one or two defenders in front of me, I generally won that battle easily. COURTESY OF AP/WIDE WORLD PHOTOS.

In 1973 I became assistant director of athletics at the University of Kansas. Yes, my Afro was in style back then!

One of my proudest moments was receiving a master's degree from Kansas in 1976.

George Halas and I were honored at Yale University in 1976 for our philanthropic efforts. Halas may have had a reputation for being tight with the dollar, but he actually helped more people financially than many realized.

Here is the 1977 Pro Football Hall of Fame class in Canton, Ohio. I am in the middle and flanked by (from the left) Forrest Gregg, Frank Gifford, Bart Starr, and Bill Willis.

Muhammad Ali and I have been involved in the Better Boys Foundation for many decades. I once lived about three blocks from Ali during my playing days with the Chicago Bears.

Tennis legend John McEnroe has a puzzled look on his face. And just think, I wasn't even officiating one of his matches! Actually, we were both in Florida for a charity event.

Ardie and I always look forward to attending the Robert Kennedy golf tournament that raises money for underprivileged nations. Ardie and I have been married 35 years.

I learned a great deal about scuba diving from Al Tomlinson, an attorney from Allentown, Pennsylvania. He is one of my best friends. Here we are preparing to dive in Belize, my favorite area.

I began scuba diving in 1981. All I asked for was "18 inches of daylight" on the football field. Scuba diving in the ocean gives me much more room to navigate. I find it a relaxing, safe, and enjoyable sport.

Muhammad Ali and his wife, Lonnie, joined us at the Drake Hotel in Chicago during a formal event that honored Ali.

The Cradle Adoption agency in Evanston, Illinois is an organization that is close to my heart. My son, Scott, is from the Cradle and I have been on that organization's board for about 20 years. Saundra Hill of the Cradle is shown here with Ardie and me.

Billy Dee Williams, who played my role in the movie Brian's Song, *appeared with me at a fundraiser in New York ten years ago. He presented me with a humanitarian award. The original 1971 cast of* Brian's Song *was scheduled to have a reunion in Chicago in September of 2007. The event will bring together the cast members from the movie for the first time since it was produced in 1971.*

Rafer Johnson, one of our country's greatest decathlon athletes, is a regular attendee at the Robert Kennedy Golf Tournament.

Renowned actor Sidney Poitier and I really related well on the golf course during this Frank Sinatra tournament in Palm Springs, California. Like me, Sidney is rather shy and understated, yet he always gets the job done.

I admire the fact that Michael Jordan donates his time and memorabilia for so many worthy causes such as this golf tournament. Both of us appreciate how Chicago fans never forget their sports heroes.

Ardie and I were all smiles when my No. 40 was retired along with Dick Butkus's No. 51 during halftime ceremonies on a stormy Halloween night in 1994 at Soldier Field. I believe the stormy weather was appropriate because 1965 was the first time two future Hall of Famers were drafted in the first round by the same team.

On June 2, 2004, I gave a speech at the Gridiron Legends Luncheon in South Bend, Indiana. During my three-year college career under Coach Jack Mitchell, I rushed for 2,675 yards, caught passes for 408 yards, and added 835 yards on kick returns to become a two-time All American. My 99-yard touchdown run as a sophomore against Nebraska is still an NCAA record. I was inducted in the College Football Hall of Fame in 1977. COURTESY OF AP/WIDE WORLD PHOTOS.

When you get to this level, I think the only thing an NFL running back has to be aware of is that he has so many more plays. I honestly don't think a coach can teach you how to run. He can teach you blocking techniques. But as far as running…I don't think so. It is difficult to change a back's running style.

If you got me the ball in an open space with just one or two defenders in front of me, I generally won that battle easily.

When I look at the 2006 Bears team, I consider Thomas Jones a better-than-good running back. When the Bears drafted Cedric Benson in 2005, they thought he was the real deal coming out of Texas. He is kind of searching for his way and injuries have slowed him. Meanwhile, Jones has stepped up his game. Jones didn't make a big deal out of Benson being around; he kept quiet and made up his mind to keep working hard. I admire that.

Jones is a very determined and relentless runner and it was hard to blame him for talking about wanting to be traded at the end of last season so he could become the featured back someplace. One thing that seems to have changed in the NFL in recent years is that almost every team relies on two or possibly even three key running backs to make it through a rigorous 16-game schedule and perhaps the playoffs. The Bears wound up trading Jones to the NY Jets in the off season for a second-round pick.

Since joining the Bears in 2004 as a free agent, Jones served as a central figure in the team's offense, rushing for a career-high 1,335 yards in 2005 while effectively thwarting the attempts of Benson to crack the starting lineup.

In addition to his impressive performances on the field, Jones has stood out with his strong work ethic and professionalism. During the Bears' bye week in the 2006 season, I read in the *Chicago Tribune* that Jones took the time to establish a scholarship fund at his alma mater. The announcement of the Thomas Quinn Jones Scholarship Fund was made in Charlottesville, Virginia, during a special event honoring the Jones family as part of the annual Family Weekend activities at the university.

My frame of thinking was always to prepare for the unexpected.

Jones, who grew up in Big Stone Gap, Virginia, received an athletic scholarship to the University of Virginia. He is one of seven children of Betty and Thomas Jones Sr., who both worked in the coal mines.

Six of the Joneses' children have attended college, including three at Virginia. The seventh is a high school senior who will enter college in 2007.

In addition to Thomas, two of his sisters, Knetris and Knetta, attended Virginia; his younger brother Julius played football at Notre Dame and is a running back with the Dallas Cowboys. And two of Jones's other sisters, Gwen and Beatrice, attended Tennessee.

"I am never going to forget where I came from because that is what made me what I am. My roots," Jones said.

He added, "I will never forget that, and I will always make sure I show my appreciation. This [scholarship] is something that is going to be there forever. It makes me feel good that I am going to be able to help someone else have the opportunity to go there."

Betty Jones worked the night shift in the coal mines to help give her children a better opportunity in life. "Both of our sons were able to use their athletic talents to gain scholarships. But football lasts a few years, and education lasts forever," she said.

Thomas added, "My mom and dad....While I was growing up, they emphasized getting A's and B's in high school and grade school. We wanted to make sure we had something to fall back on just in case football didn't work. My parents did a really good job of keeping all seven of us focused and making sure we had that same mentality."

That is the kind of attitude that I respect in an NFL player.

Of course, I am much older and hopefully wiser now when it comes to recognizing the qualities that make

I used to love small, fast sports cars, for instance. I remember owning a Corvette during my rookie year.

for a mature and conscientious professional athlete. I admit there was a time in my early years with the Bears when I was a little careless with my behavior. I used to love small, fast sports cars, for instance. I remember owning a Corvette during my rookie year. I was driving back to Chicago from Milwaukee after an exhibition game against the Packers, and I decided to see just how fast I could push it. I got up to 110 miles an hour. Unfortunately, one of the drivers I passed on the highway was Coach Halas. The next day, Halas called me into his office. He had spotted me speeding home, noticing my vanity license plate that read "GS40."

Halas said: "Gale, you know what? They could arrest you for murder."

I said: "What do you mean?"

"Well, for one thing, you were driving too fast at 110, and if you killed Linda, that would be murder. You would probably kill yourself, too. I think, my boy, you had better get rid of the Corvette."

As always, I listened to my coach and got rid of the Corvette. But then in 1967 and '68 I started scooting around town on a Honda motorbike. Again, Coach Halas found out about that and told me to get rid of it. Again, I got rid of it.

There was too much at stake to take foolish chances off the field. Coach Halas even persuaded me to stop playing on the Bears basketball team that performed during the off-season, mainly at charity events. He kept telling me that there might be some hotshot trying to prove how tough he was by injuring me on the basketball floor.

The important thing is that I responded properly to the strong suggestions of my coach.

The Bears paid me $25,000 a year during my first contract that began in 1965. Even accounting for inflation, that salary pales in comparison with what players are making today. The average NFL player's salary in 2005 was $1.4 million. The average starter was paid $2.26 million. And that does not take into account the millions of dollars star players are able to make in endorsements nowadays.

At the conclusion of my first season with the Bears, after I had scored 22 touchdowns and was named Rookie of the Year, Coach Halas gave me a check for a $10,000 bonus. I was stunned and so grateful. I had not expected anything beyond my regular salary. Even in 1968, when I missed the final five games because of the serious knee injury, he gave me a sizeable bonus.

It was small in comparison to what the players are making today, but I could not have been happier at the time.

Back when I played, we seemed to communicate with each other as players better than they do today because we didn't have much money.

Back when I played, we seemed to communicate with each other as players better than they do today because we didn't have much money. Even though almost all of the white players on the Bears lived on the North Side of Chicago and the black players lived on the South Side, nobody complained. That is just the way it was and we all got along off the field.

Regardless of who you were, there just weren't many endorsement opportunities. Today, players won't go to speak at a high school unless they get $2,500 or $5,000.

Leigh Steinberg, recognized as one of the top sports and entertainment agents in the business today, knows better than anyone else how NFL players can augment their already exorbitant salaries, especially if they are members of championship teams. Steinberg told the *Chicago Tribune* that players such as Brian Urlacher and Rex Grossman really could have struck it rich if the

Bears had won Super Bowl XLI. Not that either player is hurting for money anyway.

"I saw what happened to players I represented like Troy Aikman and Steve Young after they won Super Bowls," said Steinberg, who had Steelers quarterback Ben Roethlisberger as a client in Super Bowl XL.

"Give me one important game to win for the Bears and I would rather have Gale Sayers in my backfield."

The really big money in the NFL started to be paid in the late 1970s and '80s. Walter Payton began to benefit from that situation. Between 1976 and 1980, Payton led the NFC in rushing every season, and his annual salary rose to $475,000, the highest in the league. And, of course, he retired with the NFL's all-time rushing record, which was later broken by the Dallas Cowboys' great Emmitt Smith. If I had been able to play 13 years in the NFL like Payton did, I would have been in that range of yardage, too. As great as Walter was, many people would say, "Give me one important game to win for the Bears and I would rather have Gale Sayers in my backfield."

That is flattering for me to hear. But I had absolutely no jealousy or animosity toward Payton and we were very good friends. He was a great, great football player and he came to play every day. We both made it to the Hall of Fame, something I am very proud of.

I have nothing but the utmost respect for Payton and his family. In addition to being a great football player, Payton was a tremendous philanthropist. He organized and financed a Christmas toy drive for every child in the State of Illinois Department of Children and Family Services system because he did not want children to wake up on Christmas morning without presents. And much of his work was done anonymously for many years.

After he passed away on November 1, 1999, of cancer, I recall hearing Chicago Bears Hall of Fame linebacker Mike Singletary saying on television about Payton: "I wish there was another word I could think of other than *greatness*. That's what comes to mind. Greatness."

Virginia McCaskey, Coach Halas's daughter, already had lived through the untimely death of Brian Piccolo in 1970. "After Brian Piccolo died, my husband and I promised ourselves we wouldn't be so personally involved with the players," she said after Payton passed away. "We were able to follow that resolve until Walter Payton came into our lives."

During the week leading up to Super Bowl XLI, a "Score one for Walter" rallying cry emerged from Bears fans. Many Chicago fans would have loved to have seen a Bears player score a touchdown in the Super Bowl and then somehow acknowledge Payton's legacy. Although many of the current Bears were barely old enough to remember watching Payton perform, everyone knows that one of the greatest running backs in NFL history failed to score a touchdown in Super Bowl XX. Even defensive tackle William "Refrigerator" Perry had a goal-line carry for a touchdown in the 46–10 rout of New England.

Mike Ditka often has said he regrets not calling a play to give Payton an opportunity when the Bears were in close scoring position.

What Payton was able to accomplish on the football field and in the community will never be overlooked. He was a shining example of how to carry yourself as a high-profile athlete. Once again, as I see the exorbitant salaries paid to today's athletes, I believe it is incumbent upon them to live their lives with a sense of responsibility to society.

When NFL players like T.O. do things like that, then you start seeing it in high school and college. I just don't like it and it has nothing to do with playing football.

According to a survey printed in *USA Today*, Atlanta Falcons quarterback Michael Vick was paid over $23 million dollars, which included a $22,750,000 signing bonus, in 2005. Matt Hasselbeck, who guided the Seattle Seahawks to Super Bowl XL, was paid $19 million, including a $16 million signing bonus. Now that's a lot of zeroes for those players to be cashing! How much money do you need?

My hope is that the players today fully appreciate what financial opportunities they have, both on the field and off. And I hope and pray they don't forget the pioneers of the game who made it possible for them to take care of themselves and their families with the money they are making.

My admonishment is this: Don't destroy the game!

When I see players like Terrell Owens making all of that money and then acting foolish most of the time, it really turns me off and makes me ashamed at the way some players disrespect the game. It's a team game, simple as that. Owens has made a mockery of that. If you get pissed off and cuss out the coach, what good does that do? We are supposed to be role models.

When NFL players like T.O. do things like that, then you start seeing it in high school and college. I just don't like it and it has nothing to do with playing football. Less than 1 percent of the high school players will make it to the NFL. They need more positive role models. The crazy things players do on the field, just to be seen or to have them shown on the ESPN highlights…it's instant gratification but it is not going to help you win.

• • •

About 10 years ago, the folks at NFL Properties used to invite players from my era to go to the Super Bowl Week and spend time with business clients. We would get $5,000 or $10,000 to be with folks from Pepsi or some other company. But that practice stopped and the NFL is giving those opportunities to current players. A lot of times the current players don't even show up and fulfill their obligations because that kind of money is pocket change to them. It is so sad.

When I played, we always had to get a job during the off-season to make ends meet. I used to work at Sears Roebuck.

Should the players have made more money in my era? Well, of course, TV coverage of games wasn't a big deal then. The owners had a right to make money. It's all relative. A friend of mine now is a long-snapper for the Minnesota Vikings and he makes $425,000 a year. Just for being a long-snapper! God bless him. For the people to complain now doesn't make sense. Timing is everything in life.

I know of so many former NFL players from my era and some who played before me who are really hurting financially now because of endless medical bills and various other setbacks. Many of these pioneers played football more for the love of the game than the size of their paycheck.

Ditka and I have been campaigning heavily to improve the benefits for the pioneers of our game. During the week leading up to Super Bowl XLI, Ditka called attention to the situation. During a press conference, Ditka and fellow Hall of Famer Joe DeLamielleure blamed former commissioner Paul Tagliabue and NFL Players Association director Gene Upshaw for the current plight.

I think Gene is a good guy, a Hall of Fame player with the Oakland Raiders. But I don't think he is looking out for the players of my era.

"They were in power for 20 years and haven't done anything," DeLamielleure said at the news conference reported by the *Chicago Tribune*'s Don Pierson. "I'm passionate about this because I played next to a guy [former Bills tackle Donnie Green] for seven years who is in a homeless shelter."

Former Green Bay guard Jerry Kramer, another one of my contemporaries, announced an auction on JerryKramer.com for the Gridiron Greats Assistance Fund. Kramer is donating a Super Bowl ring. So is Ditka, although one from the Dallas Cowboys, not the 1985 Bears.

"We hope to raise a half-million dollars or so and hope to do it in the next five years," Kramer said. "I didn't realize how widespread the problem was."

Hall of Fame cornerback Lem Barney said football's pension is "the worst pension of all" the major sports. Ditka named Hall of Fame players John Mackey, Joe Perry, Doug Atkins, Jim Ringo, Pete Pihos, and Willie Wood as needing help.

"Perception is everybody who played the game does well afterward,"

For the people to complain now doesn't make sense. Timing is everything in life.

Ditka said. "I've been fortunate. I've been blessed, and I understand that and so do a lot of us. But the ones who haven't, they're not even asking. We're asking for them."

Ditka said his annual golf tournament splits proceeds between Chicago's Misericordia home and needy former NFL players.

"We don't make them jump through hoops," Ditka said. "We just give it to them."

Ditka said he had dinner during Super Bowl week with an owner in another sport he wouldn't identify. "He offered to contribute $100,000," Ditka said.

Ditka said he wrote letters to all NFL owners in 2006 asking for $100,000 apiece to create a trust fund of $3.2 million to help players in dire need.

"I don't know if the letter ever got in their hands," he said. "I got a check from one owner for $5,000 and another for $10,000, and I had our people send it back.

"I'm not trying to embarrass anybody. It's 2007. It's time to right a wrong. This has existed for a long time. [They] talk about going back and picking up the pre-1959s [players]. It's a joke. The benefit program for them was terrible."

"Perception is everybody who played the game does well afterward," Ditka said. "I've been fortunate. I've been blessed, and I understand that and so do a lot of us. But the ones who haven't, they're not even asking. We're asking for them."

The players union has a pension program for players from preunion days, but DeLamielleure said he would like to see all former players receive the same pension that current players do, which he said is $475 a month for every year of service.

"That's not asking too much," said DeLamielleure, who retired in 1985 with 13 years' service. "I took my pension at 45. My pension is $1,200-something a month. I hope gas and electricity don't go up over the next 10 years."

Upshaw said it is financially impossible to bring all retirees to the current level.

"That's never going to happen," said Upshaw, who estimated the cost of such a suggestion at $800 million.

Although the current pension is more than other industries pay, Ditka and DeLamielleure are more concerned about the suffering they see and the price players paid to build pro football into a $6-billion-a-year business.

"It's not right. And it has to stop," Ditka said. "It's not like there's not enough money to go around, because there is enough money to go around. These guys who play the game [now], not taking anything away from them, they are not the makers of the game; they are the keepers of the game. Period."

Ditka cited Mackey, a former tight end and ex-president of the NFL Players Association who needs 24-hour care because of dementia.

DeLamielleure said, "For guys who made this league and built it on their backs, their knees, their legs, and now they're all broken down and they can't even get a decent pension, it's wrong.

"I met Lou Groza when I got traded to Cleveland. His pension was $500 a month. After 22 years."

The late Groza's Hall of Fame career spanned 1946–67.

Upshaw said the union paid $1.2 million last year outside of regular benefits to 147 players with special needs. He said some players choose to take pension money early and called it unrealistic for any player to expect a pension "to take care of him for the rest of his life after he played five years and was done at age 30."

"I'm not trying to embarrass anybody. It's 2007. It's time to right a wrong. This has existed for a long time. [They] talk about going back and picking up the pre-1959s [players]."

Ditka distributed a 2001 letter from Raiders owner Al Davis to Tagliabue proposing satellite Hall of Fame sites to generate more money. Davis also suggested a permanent fund of $10 million.

Upshaw said the union is concerned about all retirees, not only Hall of Famers, and said disability issues are being discussed.

"I agree with Ditka when he says there's a lot of red tape," Upshaw said.

Troy Vincent, president of the NFLPA and current safety for the Washington Redskins, acknowledged that concern for retired players consumes much of his time, even while on the job. He said he was in a pileup on a sideline of a game and heard an assistant coach from another team yell at him, "Hey, Troy, when are you going to increase the benefits?"

In fact, I would much rather see the players make the money than some of the owners who are stuffing their pockets.

Kramer's Legends of the Game news conference and Upshaw's news conference were held at the same podium within hours of each other during Super Bowl week in Miami.

According to Jerry Kramer's website, the Gridiron Greats Assistance Fund will provide assistance to retired NFL players who are experiencing physical and financial struggles. The fund is a nonstock, nonprofit corporation that has been established to provide direct or indirect financial assistance to those retired players who are disadvantaged or indigent due to the inadequate pension and disability compensation the league provides to older players.

Once again, I do not begrudge the players of today for making the money they do. In fact, I would much rather see the players make the money than some of the owners who are stuffing their pockets. The fans are paying their salaries with expensive ticket prices, parking tabs, souvenirs, and concessions. But I think our players and the administration need to respect those who built the game.

The National Football League was established in 1920 as the American Professional Football Association with 14 teams, and the number varied each season until the 1930s when 10 teams competed. During the late 1960s when I played, the NFL had 14 teams, then grew to 16 before merging with the American Football League (AFL) expanding the number of teams to 26. Now, there are 32 teams in the NFL, once again increasing revenue sources.

According to *The Sports Industry: Football (Business Reference)*, NFL attendance has held steady at more than 61,000 per game for more than 20 years. This equates to an estimated average of 90 percent capacity for the last five years.

The NFL is now a billion-dollar business. It occupies a vast segment of the country's entertainment dollar. It is fueled by gambling, Fantasy Football fanatics, merchandise sales, and television. But to me, it always will be just a game.

Appendix A
My All-Time Bears Team

THE BEARS HAVE AN INCREDIBLE HISTORY, WITH LOTS of impressive players and performances. I thought it might be interesting to pick who I consider the greatest Bears players of all time. My apologies to any omitted fan favorites.

My coauthor, *Chicago Tribune* sports columnist Fred Mitchell, assisted in the compilation of this list, and it was at his insistence that I be placed on the first-team offense. Who am I to argue?

My All-Time Bears Team

OFFENSE		
POSITION	**NAME**	**COMMENT**
Quarterback	Sid Luckman	T-formation pioneer. Four NFL titles.
Running Back	Gale Sayers	Game's greatest open-field runner.
Running Back	Walter Payton	NFL's second all-time leading rusher.
Fullback	Bronko Nagurski	Punishing Hall of Fame runner.
Tight End	Mike Ditka	Prototype for the position.
Wide Receiver	Ken Kavanaugh	Ahead of his time.
Tackle	Jim Covert	The rock of the Super Bowl line.
Tackle	George Connor	All-NFL five times. Hall of Famer.
Guard	Stan Jones	Eight-time Pro Bowl selection. Hall of Famer.
Guard	Danny Fortmann	Hall of Famer.
Center	Clyde Turner	Six-time All-NFL. Hall of Famer.
Place-Kicker	Kevin Butler	Holds 19 club records.

DEFENSE		
POSITION	**NAME**	**COMMENT**
End	Richard Dent	Bears' all-time leading sacker.
End	Doug Atkins	Hall of Fame tough guy.
Tackle	Dan Hampton	Hall of Famer on Super Bowl squad.
Tackle	Steve McMichael	Most durable Bear.
Linebacker	Dick Butkus	Best in NFL history.
Linebacker	Otis Wilson	Fierce competitor as outside linebacker.
Linebacker	Wilber Marshall	Underrated key to Super Bowl XX team.
Cornerback	Rosey Taylor	Nine interceptions in 1963.
Cornerback	Red Grange	Two-way marvel.
Safety	Richie Petitbon	Second all-time team interception leader.
Safety	Gary Fencik	Bears' career interception leader (38).

SPECIAL TEAMS		
POSITION	**NAME**	**COMMENT**
Punter	Bobby Joe Green	Led in punting 12 straight years.
Kick Returner	Gale Sayers	Hall of Fame player. Averaged 30.6 yards a return.
Punt Returner	George McAfee	Hall of Fame swift two-way player.
Special Teams	J.C. Caroline	Matched speed and tackling ability.
Coach	George Halas	Won 324 games over 40 years.

Honorable Mention

OFFENSE	
Quarterbacks	Jim McMahon, Erik Kramer, Bill Wade, Ed Brown, George Blanda, Johnny Lujack
Running Backs/ Fullbacks	Willie Galimore, Paddy Driscoll, Neal Anderson, Rick Casares, Ronnie Bull, Jack Manders, Edward "Dutch" Sternaman, Matt Suhey, Roland Harper, Bill Osmanski, Thomas Jones
Receivers	Johnny Morris, Muhsin Muhammad, Bill Hewitt, Luke Johnsos, Jack Hoffman, Emery Moorhead, Harlon Hill, George Wilson, Dick Gordon, Wendell Davis, Jim Dooley, Willie Gault, Dennis McKinnon, Bill McColl, James Scott, Dick Plasman, Jim Keane
Tackles	Keith Van Horne, Joe Stydahar, Ed Healey, Roy Lyman, Bob Kilcullen, Bob Wetoska, Bill Bishop, Kline Gilbert, Bill Wightkin

Guards	Ray Bray, Mark Bortz, George Seals, Dick Barwegan, Tom Thayer, Ted Karras, Ruben Brown
Centers	Jay Hilgenberg, Olin Kreutz, Mike Pyle, George Trafton
Place-Kickers	Robbie Gould, Jeff Jaeger, Bob Thomas, Paul Edinger, Mac Percival, George Blanda

DEFENSE	
Ends	Ed O'Bradovich, Mike Hartenstine, Ed Sprinkle, Al Harris, Alan Page, Willie Holman
Tackles	Tommie Harris, George Musso, Fred Williams, Jim Osborne, Fred Davis, Earl Leggett, William Perry, Wally Chambers
Linebackers	Brian Urlacher, Mike Singletary, Bill George, Joe Fortunato, Lance Briggs, Doug Buffone, Larry Morris
Defensive Backs	Rosey Taylor, Erich Barnes, Donnell Woolford, Leslie Frazier, Nathan Vasher, Doug Plank, Mark Carrier, J.C. Caroline, Shaun Gayle, Allan Ellis, Dave Duerson, Todd Bell, Dave Whitsell, Mike Brown

SPECIAL TEAMS	
Punters	Maury Buford, Brad Maynard, Bob Parsons, George Gulyanics
Kick Returners	Devin Hester, Dennis Gentry, Ron Smith, Cecil Turner, Dennis McKinnon, Glynn Milburn, Steve Schubert, Ray McClean
Special Teams	Brendon Ayanbadejo, Glen Kozlowski, Maurice Douglass
Coaches	Mike Ditka, Jack Pardee, Lovie Smith

Quarterback: Sid Luckman

Luckman starred for the Bears from 1939 to 1950 and he still holds many of the franchise's passing records. He led the Bears to four NFL championships during that period.

Running Back: Gale Sayers

Running Back: Walter Payton

The Bears drafted Payton in the first round, as the fourth overall pick in 1975 out of Jackson State.

Payton rushed for 16,726 career yards and scored 110 touchdowns. He set several team records, including most career rushing yards and touchdowns. Additionally, his jersey number was retired, and he was inducted into the Pro Football Hall of Fame in 1993.

Former Cowboys running back Tony Dorsett was watching television in the den of his Dallas home when he saw Payton's press conference disclosing his life-threatening liver disease in 1999.

"It was very touching," Dorsett, a 1994 Pro Football Hall of Fame inductee, told the *Chicago Tribune*. "I was just a big admirer of Walter Payton, the person. I almost broke down myself."

Payton always had kept himself in top physical condition, but there was a sign of liver trouble eight years prior to his death in 1999.

"In 1991, when he had a road-racing problem, at that time he was found to have abnormal liver enzymes. Even under a liver biopsy, it seemed to resolve on its own. In that respect, he probably was already affected with the disease. So, he got better by himself. In retrospective, it was probably there," Dr. Joseph Lagattuta was quoted as saying by the Associated Press.

In addition to playing football, Payton had an affinity for fast cars and fancy guns.

Fullback: Bronko Nagurski

Bronko Nagurski was one of the first football players to succeed as a professional wrestler. In professional wrestling, he was a world heavyweight champion.

According to the Pro Football Hall of Fame, his parents were ethnic Ukrainians from the Polish Ukraine. Nagurski played fullback on offense and tackle on defense and was named an All-American at Minnesota.

Nagurski retired from pro football in 1937 after eight seasons to pursue a more profitable pro wrestling career. He returned to the Bears in 1943 when the team was short of players during World War II.

Tight End: Mike Ditka

There's much more to Da Coach than his Hall of Fame ring, gruff persona, and *Saturday Night Live* caricature. Ditka is committed to charities and he has a soft spot in his heart for helping needy children.

"I think you have to give back. I got involved with Misericordia years ago, and I wouldn't change that [decision] for anything," Ditka said in a *Chicago Tribune* interview.

"I have met some wonderful people who have enriched my life. It's not what you give, it's what you get. And these kids love unconditionally because they don't know anything else. That's their mentality; that's what they are all about. Whether you are helping to cure heart disease or cancer or whatever, they are all a worthwhile cause. But when you are talking about children, that becomes that much more significant to me because they haven't had a chance to live. They haven't had a chance to do what we've done. We have had full lives, and we will be able to look back and reflect on this and that. But the most important thing to me is to make sure the children have a fair opportunity to experience what we have experienced."

It concerns Ditka that so many younger professional athletes today appear so self-centered and unwilling to give of their time and money to assist worthwhile causes—that they just don't seem to get it.

"If they don't get it, then that's their problem. Look at the guys who do get it," said Ditka. "Emmitt Smith gets it. Walter Payton got it. I mean, there are a lot of guys who get it. Jerry Rice gets it. There are a lot of guys who get it. So don't say that you don't get it because you are young. You don't get it because you don't care. And if you don't care, eventually people are not going to care about you.

"Part of our lives we are in the parade. And then the rest of our lives we kind of watch the parade. When you start watching the parade, people quit caring about you. Then you find out what it's all about."

Wide Receiver: Ken Kavanaugh
Ken Kavanaugh, who played college football at LSU, starred with the Bears, but his career was interrupted by World War II, during which he was a pilot.

He set the Bears record of 13 touchdown receptions in a season, a mark that was later tied by Dick Gordon. Kavanaugh also set the mark for the highest average gain per reception in a career of 22.4 yards. He averaged 25.6 yards a catch in 1947.

Hired by the New York Giants in 1955 as an assistant coach, Kavanaugh continued in that position until 1971 when he became a scout for the Giants. He retired from football in 1999 and died of complications from pneumonia on January 25, 2007, in Sarasota, Florida.

Tackle: Jim Covert

Jim Covert was an All-Pro offensive tackle for the Bears. He was a two-time All-American at Pitt.

In 1983 he was selected as the sixth pick of the first round. Named to the NFL 1980s All-Decade Team, Covert was the Bears' offensive captain along with Payton. He was selected to the Pro Bowl twice and he also was a key member of the Super Bowl XX championship squad. He retired following the 1990 season due to back injuries.

The Bears led the league in rushing in 1977 behind the running of Payton, and then did not lead the league in that category again until Covert's rookie year of '83. The entire offensive line of Jay Hilgenberg at center, Tom Thayer and Mark Bortz at guards, and Covert and Keith Van Horne at the tackles remained intact for seven years. That continuity was important to the Bears' success.

"Yeah, that was pretty amazing. We led the league in rushing four straight years," recalled Covert in a *Chicago*

Tribune article. "Fans today have to be true pro football fans to keep up with all this player movement throughout the league. I played my entire career with one team and I had several teammates who did."

Covert likely would have to play guard instead of tackle in today's game.

"Probably. My rookie year I came in at 290 pounds and Coach Ditka wanted me down to 275. He said he thought that was the weight that I played my best football."

Tackle: George Connor

George Connor starred for the Bears from 1948 to 1955 as an offensive tackle and a linebacker. He was originally a number one draft pick by the New York Giants in 1946.

He earned All-NFL recognition on both offense and defense.

A Chicago native, Connor's career was cut short by a knee injury after the 1955 season. He played in four Pro Bowls (1950–53).

Guard: Stan Jones

Stan Jones is a Pro Football Hall of Famer who starred as both a guard on offense and as a defensive tackle. He played for the Bears from 1954 to 1965 and for the Washington Redskins in 1966. So I had an opportunity to play with Jones in my rookie year of 1965.

He missed only two games his first 11 seasons, was an All-NFL guard in 1955, 1956, 1959, and 1960, and played in seven straight Pro Bowls.

Jones was one of the first pro football players to concentrate on a weight-lifting program to build him into playing condition.

Guard: Danny Fortmann

A ninth-round pick in the 1936 draft out of Colgate, Fortmann became the youngest starter in the NFL at the age of 20. It was the first year of the NFL draft.

A brilliant student who was Phi Beta Kappa at Colgate, Fortmann earned a medical degree while playing in the NFL. He was either first- or second-team All-NFL every season of his career.

Center: Clyde Turner

Clyde "Bulldog" Turner excelled as a center and linebacker. He was the Bears' number one draft pick in 1940 and was a rookie starter at the age of 20 following a Little All-America career at Hardin-Simmons.

At 6′1″, 237 pounds, Turner led the NFL with eight interceptions in 1942. He had 17 interceptions over his career. Turner was All-NFL seven times and he intercepted four passes in five NFL title games. Turner excelled as a center and linebacker for the Bears for 13 seasons.

Place-Kicker: Kevin Butler

Selected as the Bears' fourth-round pick in the 1985 draft out of Georgia, Butler set 19 club records in 11 seasons and remains the Bears' all-time leading scorer.

In 1989, he set a then-NFL record of 24 consecutive field goals. Bears Pro Bowl kicker Robbie Gould broke that club record in 2006.

At Georgia, Butler kicked a 60-yard field goal to beat Clemson. He became the first pure kicker to be elected to the College Football Hall of Fame. With the Bears, Butler set an NFL rookie scoring record with 144 points (breaking my mark) in 1985 when he kicked 31 field goals and 51 extra points for the Super Bowl XX champions.

Butler finished his career with the Arizona Cardinals in 1997, retiring with 1,208 points, sixth most in NFL history among kickers.

End: Richard Dent

Dent was sacked again in the final balloting for the Pro Football Hall of Fame in January 2007, but I feel he deserves to one day be inducted.

The Super Bowl XX MVP and the Bears' all-time leader in quarterback sacks sounded exasperated and frustrated after learning his bid fell short.

"I am not shocked, I am not surprised. To me, this shows disrespect for what I have accomplished and what I have done," Dent told the *Chicago Tribune*. "There are certain things that I have no control over and I try not to concern myself with that. I don't know what the process [for Hall of Fame selection] is. But this disappointment is something I have been dealing with since I was 21 years old. It is no different for me now at the age of 46."

The Hall of Fame selection committee pared the list from 17 to 11, then from 11 to six, with the final six receiving yes or no votes for the Hall of Fame. Dent, in his fifth year of eligibility, was on the list of 11 but failed to make the cut to six.

All six finalists—former Browns offensive lineman Gene Hickerson, Cowboys wide receiver Michael Irvin, Oilers and Titans offensive lineman Bruce Matthews, Lions tight end Charlie Sanders, Bills running back Thurman Thomas, and Cardinals defensive back Roger Wehrli—made the Hall of Fame.

Dent, an eighth-round draft pick out of Tennessee State in 1983, was a four-time Pro Bowl selection who also played for the 49ers, Colts, and Eagles. He wound up his 15-year career with 137.5 sacks, eight interceptions, 13 fumble recoveries, and two touchdowns. In 1985, Dent recorded 17 sacks, intercepted two passes, and recovered two fumbles. Between 1984 and 1985, Dent recorded 34½ sacks.

"At the age of 23, to come into this league and do what I did...if they are not in your camp, it doesn't make any difference," said Dent.

Dent's former teammates Payton, Singletary, and Hampton already have been enshrined in the Pro Football Hall of Fame.

"I know what I did on the field and what I accomplished," said Dent. "I just live off that."

End: Doug Atkins

They didn't record a music video for posterity like the '85 Bears did, but the 1963 NFL champion Bears were pretty remarkable.

As the Super Bowl XX Bears commemorated the 20th anniversary of their stellar season in 2005, one Hall of Fame member of the '63 champions wondered, "What about us?"

Atkins, who was a 6′8″, 280-pound stalwart, told the *Chicago Tribune* from his home in Knoxville, Tennessee, "When all the Super Bowls started, people just kind of forgot about us. Like that era is off the charts."

Atkins played 17 seasons in the NFL, 12 with the Bears, after being selected in the first round out of Tennessee by the Cleveland Browns. The eight-time Pro Bowl selection played in an era when head slaps and late hits on the quarterback were not subject to review, scrutiny, or penalty.

"If I used a head slap, it wasn't intentional," said Atkins. "In the old days, it didn't matter where you hit 'em. They have softened the game up. And I don't think the officials are as good as they used to be."

Atkins acknowledges the accomplishments of the '85 Bears, but he says the '63 world champs' defense should receive more recognition than it has.

"We had three outstanding linebackers in Joe Fortunato, [Hall of Famer] Bill George, and Larry Morris," he said. "On the defensive line we had Ed O'Bradovich, Stan Jones, Fred Williams, Bob Kilcullen, and myself. And our four defensive backs had [36] interceptions."

The 1963 team, which beat the New York Giants 14–10 in the NFL championship game at Wrigley Field, allowed the fewest touchdowns in franchise history with 18. They allowed 144 points in 14 games (10.3 per game), while the '85 Bears defense allowed 198 points in 16 regular-season games (12.4 per game).

"I think we might have beat [the '85 Bears] by a point or two," said Atkins, 76, who feels the NFL game has changed significantly since he played.

"It looks like a bunch of sumo wrestlers at the line of scrimmage nowadays," he said. "They get engaged in their blocks and they are all hugging and stuff. I don't know why they can't use a head slap anymore."

Atkins said his highest base salary with the Bears was $25,000 with a $5,000 signing bonus. When he wound up his career with the New Orleans Saints, he made $53,000.

"They are making more money now than they can spend," he said. "Also, the whole attitude of the league has changed as far as discipline. There are too many clowns. Every day you read about them beating up a woman or running over a person and then getting another chance. Don't know what you have to do to go to jail anymore. They are a bunch of scum-bums."

Tackle: Dan Hampton

Hampton, part of the fearsome defense that carried the Bears to the 1985 NFL title, played both end and tackle from 1979 to 1990. The fourth overall pick in the 1979 draft, he fought off injuries throughout his career to rank among the most dangerous pass rushers and run stoppers in the league.

Hampton was an All-American at the University of Arkansas and was named the Southwestern Conference Defensive Player of the Year as a senior.

"Jimmy Johnson was the guy who recruited me [at Arkansas] and coached me my first two years. Frank Broyles, and then Lou Holtz came in," he told the *Chicago Tribune* after his Hall of Fame induction. "Then [with the Bears] it was Mike Ditka and Buddy Ryan. I can't tell you how much [former Bears defensive line coach] Dale Haupt meant to me because he was such a taskmaster. We played every rattin' down. I never came off the field. Guys today play five plays and raise their hand and come out for five."

In 1985, the Bears' defensive front included Hampton, William "Refrigerator" Perry, Steve McMichael, and Dent, who had 17 sacks that season.

By 1988, Al Harris was starting at left defensive end and Hampton was moved inside to tackle. Hampton was able to practice just a few days a week at that point because so much of the cartilage had been surgically removed from his knees. But he contributed big plays on game day, often blocking extra points and field goals on special teams assignments or deflecting passes at the line of scrimmage.

"John Levra [former defensive assistant coach] was a technical guy. When I started getting beat up at the end, he showed me a lot of ways to kind of avoid the bad steps and still be able to play," he said.

"I blocked three or four a year. Buddy Ryan made us take great pride in it. Alan Page, as great as he was, had great technique and he showed me a lot about blocking kicks."

Hampton wound up his career in 1990, having played 157 games.

"The attitude that Dan brought to the game was incredible," said Mike Singletary. "The next thing is the value that he had on the team. He was the leading force.

Without Dan it would have been very difficult for us to do what we did as a defense. He made all the difference in the world."

Singletary and fellow linebackers Otis Wilson and Wilber Marshall were able to maneuver more effectively because of the stellar line play in front of them. When Marshall departed the Bears, linebackers Ron Rivera and Jim Morrissey became effective. The domino effect carried over into the secondary, where cornerbacks Mike Richardson and Leslie Frazier and safeties Dave Duerson and Gary Fencik were free to roam.

"Dan and Steve McMichael complemented each other very well. The strength of any team is on the inside. If you cannot penetrate the inside of the defense, you have problems," said Singletary.

Hampton wonders if the fact that there were so many outstanding Bears defensive players might hurt the chances of other teammates making the Hall of Fame.

"All I see is all of these Steelers [five defensive players from the former Super Bowl championship teams of the '70s] who keep getting in. And you look at the stats and our defenses were, I think, quite a bit more effective than they were," said Hampton. "Winning Super Bowls has a huge bearing on who goes in the Hall of Fame. I think that's unfortunate."

Ryan introduced the revolutionary "46 defense" that became the dominant scheme in the mid-1980s. Singletary feels the effectiveness of those Bears defenses has been understated because the Bears made it to only one Super Bowl.

"It's unfortunate. I heard a commentator say recently that the '46 defense' was unconventional. And that there was just a short stretch that it was effective. Give us the credit we are due. We won football games week in and week out," said Singletary. "We had so many players banged up down the stretch—like [quarterback] Jim McMahon—that we just didn't have it."

The Bears had an 85–29 record when Hampton was healthy enough to play during his 12-year career. They were 8–16 when he did not play.

"It kind of embarrasses me because I didn't want to miss any games. I think I missed like [24] games over my career," said Hampton. "Obviously, with 12 knee operations you are not going to play every down every game. Maybe I was smart and got hurt [before] facing the good teams, I don't know."

Hampton insists the journey to the Hall of Fame was more satisfying than getting there.

Tackle: Steve McMichael

The durable defensive tackle on the Super Bowl XX team was proud of his stamina during his 15-year career.

"I never missed a game [he played 191 in a row]. I have a greater appreciation, and people should have a greater appreciation of me because of how long I played the game," he told the *Chicago Tribune*.

"It's a yearlong job. You work out hard. You don't get all those little injuries. I think this is where these new kids are missing the boat. You want to relax and take it easy, but after you get out of the game and you look back on it, you say to yourself: 'Man, that happened so fast. Why didn't I do more?' You're going to look in the mirror one of these days and you aren't going to like the person you see in it."

McMichael always had a daredevil side to him. "Before I was a football player, I was a jumper. I liked to jump off of things," he said. "That was kind of a precursor to going out on the field and throwing your body around. When I was four years old, I put a ladder on the side of the house. I got on top of the house with an umbrella. I was going to see if I could fly down. I went down a little bit too fast."

The Texas native always knew he would play football for a living. "We lived in Pasadena, Texas, just south of the Astrodome," he said. "They were just putting up the girders; they were just starting to build it. I asked my parents, 'What is that?' And of course they said they were building a football stadium. That was my first rec-ollection that there was such a thing as football. And I ended up playing a high school All-Star Game in the Astrodome. Then in college [at the University of Texas], I played in the Astrodome against the Houston Cougars. In the NFL with the Bears, I played against the Oilers in the Astrodome. It was like destiny. I was one of the few guys in the history of high school sports to make All-State three ways. One of those was as a kicker. I also ran the ball in high school and played on the line."

McMichael began his pro career with the New England Patriots. "Nobody has ever seen me in a New England Patriots uniform," he said. "New England labeled me 'the criminal element in the league.' You know how I was in practice. And they had heard the stories about me running around in the combat zone in Boston. And they knew there were some practices where I didn't get any sleep the night before. So they called me up to the office and said, 'We're releasing you because we think you are the criminal element of the league.' But it was not a bad thing, because then I came to the Bears.

"I think Papa Bear [George Halas] was a violent person. I think he knew that kind of went hand in hand with playing football. Especially down in the trenches. You have to be violent. You can't be smooth and mechanical."

McMichael doubts anyone will ever see a front seven on defense like the Super Bowl champion unit that included McMichael, Hampton, Perry, Dent, Singletary, Wilson, and Marshall.

"Our front seven guys would have started on any team in the league and been a star. It was a point in time when all of the planets aligned, to have that many great guys to be on one defense. And that many characters who were unabashed. It was a total package for a sportswriter, a golden age. Mike Ditka called the defensive line group that used to go out and have drinks 'the Night Riders.'"

It took a while before McMichael could impress his Bears defensive coordinator Buddy Ryan.

"New England had cut me and it was six weeks into the season when the Bears called me up to replace an injured defensive lineman," he said. "Well, [veteran] Alan Page never practiced. So I realized that first day that I was going to have every play of that practice. Before the practice started, Buddy Ryan came up to me and said, 'Hey,

No. 76, we're going to work your butt off today. Have you been staying in shape?' I said, 'Yeah, I've got this big black Great Dane. And me and him have been jogging.' After practice I am bent over and gassed after wind sprints. And I could hear Ryan coming up from behind me saying, 'Shoot, No. 76, we should have signed the dog.'"

Linebacker: Dick Butkus

Dick Butkus joined the Bears as a first-round draft pick in 1965, the same year I joined the team. He was elected to the Pro Football Hall of Fame in 1979, his first year of eligibility.

Butkus told the *Chicago Tribune* how Halas managed to get him worked up before games. "I always had a strong desire to play well against the Lions," he said. "Early on in my career, I was working on my snaps during pregame warm-ups, because I snapped for the punts. Halas just walked by me and said: 'Hey, did you hear what Flanagan said about you?' Ed Flanagan was Detroit's center. I said: 'No, what did he say?'

"And Halas just walked away. He just wanted to start a rivalry. He had a way to pull your chain."

Butkus, now a successful television and movie actor, is not convinced he likes all of the changes in today's NFL game. "They keep talking about all the innovations and everything else. But it still comes down to the players actually having the desire to put out on the field," he said. "It just seems that as the years go by, you kind of question that. It is a team game, and the way people carry on and make it an individual sport is beyond me why they want to bring attention to themselves. But everybody does it, so it is not that different anymore. In our era, if any kind of individual celebrations were done, our guys certainly would have taken care of that."

Butkus had some well-documented disputes with Halas over contract issues and injury settlements. "I was just thinking about how it was when we had to negotiate with him. He would say, 'I don't know what you think, but everybody comes here to watch Gale Sayers play, not you.' Then I talked to Gale later and he would say that Halas said to him: 'They are not coming to see you, they are coming to see Butkus.'"

Butkus appreciated Halas's pioneering effort to start a new professional league, handling the business end as well as the coaching. "He did everything himself and he owned it himself, along with a few people," said Butkus. "It wasn't like he came in with all of this extra money from some other business or whatever. He was one of the true guys like the Rooneys and the Maras and owners like that. They were flying by the seat of their pants. You have to understand that. A lot of people might have got upset about it, the players and everything else. But when you think back, if you run any type of business, that is the way you have got to do it to be successful. Sometimes you just question how other ownerships are coming in now and doing it to twirl umbrellas on the sidelines and stuff like that. It's just a different game now."

Butkus also gained an appreciation for Halas's nego-tiating strategy. "Everybody would talk about how cheap he was, but later on you would find out about all the people he would really help. He never let it be known," said Butkus. "I think he was great for the game, great for the league. And having been from Chicago myself [Chicago Vocational High School] and playing for the founder of football, it was neat. He was a no b.s. guy. That's the way I was brought up. And I think we hit it off great. One minute he would be yelling at you and the next minute he would be patting you on the back."

Linebacker: Otis Wilson

During his heyday as a bruising linebacker for the Super Bowl XX champion Bears, Otis Wilson was known for his relentless tackling and determination on the football field. The self-proclaimed "Junk Yard Dog" gave substance and attitude to a stellar linebacking crew that included Mike Singletary and Wilber Marshall.

Wilson was picked in the first round of the 1980 draft by the Bears from Louisville. He was a solid, fast outside linebacker whose skills improved with the addition of the streaking Marshall and the steadily improving Singletary. In 1984, the year the team set an NFL record with 72 quarterback sacks, Wilson compiled 6.5. And 1984 was the year he began to stand out. With Al Harris manning the other outside linebacker spot, the Bears became almost impossible to run or pass against.

Against Minnesota at Soldier Field in 1985, Wilson grabbed one of five interceptions on the day and took it in for a score. Against Dallas, in a 44–0 blowout, Wilson also was a major force. He recorded 10½ sacks that year.

Wilson wrote those memorable lyrics for the "Super Bowl Shuffle":

> *I'm mama's boy Otis, one of a kind.*
> *The ladies all love me for my body and my mind.*
> *I'm slick on the floor as I can be.*
> *But ain't no sucker gonna get past me.*
> *Some guys are jealous of my style and class,*
> *That's why some end up on their ———,*
> *I didn't come here lookin' for trouble,*
> *I just get down to the Super Bowl Shuffle.*

In 1987, Wilson injured his knee and seemed to fall out of favor with Ditka during the players' strike. He was cut in 1988 after eight stellar years with the Bears, playing one more year with the Los Angeles Raiders.

Now, more than 20 years later, Wilson is helping Chicago's youth tackle problems involving their general health, fitness, nutrition, and self-esteem.

"I work with a group called ASC—Athletic Sports Camps," said Wilson in an interview with *Chicago Sports Profiles*. "We do hard-core football camps and we are probably in six to eight cities across the country. And we work with young men from the ages of eight to 18 in contact football. After doing that for a number of years, I have noticed a trend in athletes. Their mind-set was: 'We have to get as big as we can and as strong as we can.' But ultimately, they weren't being fit enough. These guys would be huge, but fat and overweight and pretty much out of shape."

Wilson said he would watch the youngsters in the cafeteria of these football camps and noticed their eating habits were atrocious. The camps would provide nutritious food in the camps, but many of the young men would settle for the quickie snacks and bypass the fruit and vegetables.

"At that point I said to myself, 'Let me really start carving out a niche here and help these young men get physically fit.' I wanted to get them straight mentally, physically, and spiritually so that they could focus on nutrition and sports. That is what I call the total package."

With that plan in mind, Wilson went to work to try to change attitudes and habits when it comes to conditioning the bodies of young people. Wilson added a program to his personal foundation called "55 Alive." The program centered on fitness and nutrition for young men and women from ages seven to 17 in summer camps. He began working with young people in the Bellwood, Illinois, community, realizing that obesity among America's youth has become a serious issue.

Wilson has approached Illinois Gov. Rod Blagojevich in an effort to get his support for the fitness initiative. The dialogue continues with the governor. "And the good thing is that he hasn't said no. So some good things might happen down the road," said Wilson.

Wilson then took his idea to Chicago Mayor Richard Daley, who suggested he get involved in the Chicago Public School's "After School Matters" program.

"Mayor Daley said: 'This would be a great vehicle to give more credibility to your foundation,'" Wilson recalled. He now has access to 35 schools and aspires to be in every Chicago public school.

The multifaceted sports component of the "After School Matters" program includes an opportunity for young students to learn how to become scorekeepers, timers, and lifeguards. Wilson decided to add the fitness aspect to that program, as well as the sports and coaching features during an eight-week session.

After an 18-week period of training these high school students, Wilson plans to have the youngsters visit an adjacent middle school and have the high schoolers mentor and train the younger kids.

"What I like about this idea is that you are teaching these high school students how to be responsible," said Wilson. "And you have given them some job skills as a referee or a coach or a personal trainer."

Wilson later went to the Kinesiology Department at the University of Illinois–Chicago and encouraged them to become a part of his program, as well. His goal is to have college students working with high school students and high school students with middle school kids with the emphasis on fitness, nutrition, and sports.

"It's not just about baseball, basketball, or football. My motto is: 'Make the right life choices. Eat healthy, stay active, and help somebody else,'" he said.

Wilson has been involved in this mission for the past several years. "I am really excited about it because we started out in two schools and now we are in 16 schools, with access to 35 schools," he said.

Wilson is not insisting that these youngsters become well-conditioned athletes as he was during his younger days, but he is challenging them to eat healthy, stay active, and make sound choices.

"Just like you feed that brain, you have to feed those muscles," said Wilson. "I have been blessed with a great career. Chicago has been great to me. I love what I am doing here. And working with these young kids helps me pass on my experiences."

Linebacker: Wilber Marshall

Wilber Marshall was born April 18, 1962, in Titusville, Florida. He played linebacker for the Bears, the Washington Redskins, the Houston Oilers, the Arizona Cardinals, and the New York Jets. He won two Super Bowls as a member of the 1985 Bears and Super Bowl XXVI with the 1991 Redskins. He was named to the Pro Bowl following the 1986, 1987, and 1992 seasons.

Marshall was a member of the Florida Gators football team and was named National Defensive Player of the Year in 1983 by *ABC Sports*. He was an All-American and a finalist for the Lombardi Award in both 1982 and 1983. In 1999, Florida named Marshall a first-team selection to the Team of the Century, and also named Marshall the Defensive Player of the Century. He made the College Football All-America Team twice (1982, 1983) and left Florida with 343 tackles and a school record 23 sacks.

Marshall is perhaps best known as a member of the 1985 Bears. In the NFC championship game, against the Los Angeles Rams, he came through in magnificent fashion. At the beginning of the fourth quarter, snow began to fall at Soldier Field. On the next play, Dent sacked Rams quarterback Dieter Brock, causing Brock to fumble. Marshall picked up the loose football and ran 52 yards through the falling snow for a clinching score.

The Bears beat the Rams 24–0, and Marshall's fumble return for a touchdown continues to be the most replayed highlight from that game. FOX News Chicago named that play the most iconic moment of the game. Marshall also had a good performance in the Super Bowl, recording a sack and recovering a fumble.

Marshall won another championship ring with the Redskins in the 1991 season, when they beat the Buffalo Bills 37–24 in Super Bowl XXVI, and Marshall finished the game with several tackles and a sack. Two weeks before that, he had a superb performance in the Redskins' 41–10 win over the Detroit Lions, sacking Detroit quarterback Erik Kramer three times.

In his 12 NFL seasons, Marshall recorded 45 sacks and intercepted 23 passes, which he returned for 304 yards and three touchdowns. He also recovered 16 fumbles, returning them for 70 yards and one touchdown.

Unfortunately, Marshall's career ended with numerous debilitating injuries. Permanently disabled, Marshall's days of battling other players have been replaced with days of fighting with the NFL and the players union over a settlement pertaining to his injuries. Mike Ditka has aided in Marshall's fight by forming a coalition to raise additional awareness.

Marshall was asked by the *Chicago Tribune*'s Melissa Isaacson in early 2007 how old he feels today. The 44-year-old Marshall did not hesitate.

"A hundred," he said.

Marshall lives in Virginia, on permanent disability from the NFL. He has had both knees and a shoulder replaced and has a degenerative disc in his neck, nerve impairments in both arms, and chronic pain from ankles that were broken four times. He will need knee-replacement surgery again someday as well as surgery on both hips and shoulders.

"Besides that," Marshall added, "is the stress that goes along with it because there's nothing you can do and the NFL doesn't take care of its players."

Marshall is like many of his contemporaries waging battles with the NFL and the players union over disability benefits. He was a highly paid player of his generation, leaving the Bears after the 1987 season for a five-year, $6 million offer to play for Washington. (The Bears declined to match it but received the Redskins' first-round draft picks in 1988 and 1989 as compensation.) Now Marshall says the biggest luxury money affords him is the ability to pay for legal expenses.

Marshall is very careful about what he puts in his body, he says. The pain is "bad" but would be worse if not for "a medicine case any druggie would love." He walks with a limp and weighs 270 pounds, in large part, he says, because his injuries make it hard to work out.

"If I even tried, they'd say you're trying to do this exercise, so you're not disabled," he says.

He did not attend the 20th reunion of the Bears' Super Bowl season, he says, because of a financial dispute with the team, since settled.

Cornerback: Rosey Taylor

Along with fellow cornerback Bennie McRae, veteran Roosevelt Taylor was a key performer on the 1963 NFL champion Bears. Taylor, a two-time Pro Bowl selection, recorded a league-high nine interceptions in 1963.

A product of Grambling State, Taylor also was an adept punt and kickoff return artist. He finished his NFL career with the San Francisco 49ers and Washington Redskins after playing nine years with the Bears.

The Bears beat the New York Giants 14–10 in the NFL championship game on a frigid December afternoon at Wrigley Field in 1963. That was two years before I would be drafted out of the University of Kansas.

Cornerback: Harold "Red" Grange

George Halas was desperately seeking a special gate attraction to help draw attention not only to the Bears but also to the National Football League as a whole in the early 1920s.

University of Illinois running back Harold "Red" Grange, nicknamed the "Galloping Ghost," appeared to be the solution. The 6′, 180-pound Grange was a charter inductee to the Pro Football Hall of Fame in 1963. Born June 13, 1903, in Forksville, Pennsylvania, Grange died January 28, 1991, at the age of 87.

Safety: Richie Petitbon

Richie Petitbon was a terrific safety for the 1963 NFL championship game, intercepting a pass in the waning seconds to preserve a 14–10 victory over the New York Giants at Wrigley Field.

Petitbon joined the Bears after playing college football at Tulane University. He starred for the Bears from 1959 to 1968, the Los Angeles Rams in 1969 and 1970, and the Washington Redskins in 1971 and 1972.

Safety: Gary Fencik

Fencik finished his pro career with 38 interceptions, which he returned for 488 yards and a touchdown. He also recorded two sacks and recovered 14 fumbles, returning them for 65 yards.

Fencik played 12 seasons with the Bears and is their all-time leader in interceptions and total tackles. He was the team's defensive captain through the 1980s including the 1985 Super Bowl championship season. He made two Pro Bowl appearances (1980, 1981). He was also awarded a gold record and a platinum video award for the 1985 "Super Bowl Shuffle."

He played college football at Yale University, where he received his bachelor's degree in 1976. In 1985, he received an MBA from Northwestern University. He was also a Rhodes scholar.

Punter: Bobby Joe Green

The art of the coffin-corner kick was mastered by Bobby Joe Green, who controlled those high spirals with incredible precision. Green led the Bears in punting for 12 seasons from 1962 to 1973. During the Bears' championship season of 1963, Green averaged a Bears career-best 46.5 yards a boot.

A product of the University of Florida, Green still holds the Bears record for career yards punting (35,057) and season average (46.5). Green was selected for the Pro Bowl team in 1970.

Kick Returner: Gale Sayers

I am very proud of the fact that I still own the NFL career record for kickoff return average at 30.6 yards. People often asked me if I was ever scared to return kicks, knowing that 11 defenders had a running start and were trying to take my head off.

The answer is that I was never scared. Once again, with my excellent peripheral vision, I felt comfortable knowing that once I caught the kick, I could elude most tacklers in a one-on-one situation. That's where my "18 inches of daylight" quote comes into play. My theory was that the more times I could touch the football—whether on a punt, kickoff, pass reception, or run from scrimmage—the better the chances were that I could break one for a touchdown.

I enjoyed those moments and prided myself on believing that no defender could deliver a straight-on, full-force tackle on me. Believe me, they tried.

Punt Returner: George McAfee

At 6′, 178 pounds, halfback George McAfee was not an imposing physical presence. But Halas traded three players to the Philadelphia Eagles shortly after they made the Duke All-American their number one draft choice in 1940.

McAfee scored 234 points, gained 5,313 combined net yards, and intercepted 25 passes in eight seasons. He was the NFL punt return champion in 1948, and his career punt return average was 12.8 yards.

A member of the 1966 Pro Football Hall of Fame class, McAfee returned a punt 75 yards for a touchdown with just seconds remaining to defeat the Brooklyn Dodgers in his first exhibition game.

Special Teams: J.C. Caroline

Known as "Mr. Zoom," J.C. Caroline led the nation in rushing as a sophomore in 1953 and was named All-American at the University of Illinois. In nine games he gained 1,256 yards by rushing, 52 on pass receptions, 129 on punt returns, and 233 in kickoff returns.

A member of the College Football Hall of Fame, Caroline went to the Bears and played 10 years, starring as a defensive back.

Caroline finished his career with 24 interceptions and six total touchdowns (two rushing, one receiving, one fumble recovery, and two on interceptions).

Coach: George Halas

Perhaps the best way to describe my former coach with the Bears is to simply recall one of his favorite quotes: "Nothing is work unless you'd rather be doing something else."

He loved what he did and it showed with all of his pioneering efforts in the NFL.

Appendix B
Gale Eugene Sayers:
The Essential Facts

- Born: May 30, 1943, Wichita, Kansas

- Two-time All-American at Kansas University, class of 1965

- 3,917 college all-purpose yards, including 2,675 yards rushing

- Selected in the first round of 1965 AFL draft by Kansas City Chiefs

- Selected in the first round of 1965 NFL draft by Chicago Bears

- Set NFL rookie record with 22 touchdowns and 132 points scored, 1965

- Named 1965 NFL Rookie of the Year

- Led NFL in rushing: 1966 and 1969

- Led NFL in rushing attempts: 1969

- Led NFL in kickoff returns, 1965 and 1966

- Selected All-Pro: 1965, 1966, 1967, 1968, 1969

- Named to Pro Bowl: 1965, 1966, 1967, 1969

- Pro Bowl Most Valuable Player: 1966, 1967, 1969

- Holds all-time NFL record with 30.6 yards per kick-off return

- Youngest player elected to Pro Football Hall of Fame: 1977

- Named to NFL's 1960s All-Decade Team: 1995

- Named to NFL's 75th Anniversary All Star Team: 1995

College Statistics at Kansas University

RUSHING				
YEAR	ATT	YDS	AVG	TD
1962	158	1125	7.1	7
1963	132	917	6.9	8
1964	122	633	5.2	4
Totals	**448**	**2675**	**6.0**	**19**

100 YARD GAMES
11
Career Best: 283 yds. vs. Oklahoma State
September 22, 1962

LONGEST RUNS		
99 yds.	vs. Nebraska	November 9, 1963
96 yds.	vs. Oklahoma State	October 27, 1962
81 yds.	vs. Wyoming	October 3, 1964

KICKOFF RETURNS				
YEAR	RET	YDS	AVG	TD
1962	6	141	23.5	0
1963	9	184	20.4	0
1964	7	195	27.9	1
Totals	**22**	**520**	**23.6**	**1**

LONGEST RETURN		
93 yds.	vs. Oklahoma	October 17, 1964

Professional Football Statistics
with the Chicago Bears

		RUSHING						RECEIVING			
YEAR	GP	ATT	YDS	AVG	LG	TD	REC	YDS	AVG	LG	TD
1965	14	166	867	5.2	61	14	29	507	17.5	80	6
1966	14	229	1231*	5.4	58	8	34	447	13.1	80	2
1967	13	186	880	4.7	70	7	16	126	7.9	32	1
1968	9	138	856	6.2*	63	2	15	117	7.8	21	0
1969	14	236*	1032*	4.4	28	8	17	116	6.8	25	0
1970	2	23	52	2.3	15	0	1	-6	-6	-6	0
1971	2	13	38	2.9	9	0	0	0	0	0	0
Totals	68	991	4956	5.0	70	39	112	1307	11.7	80	9

		PUNT RETURNS						KICKOFF RETURNS			
YEAR	GP	RET	YDS	AVG	LG	TD	RET	YDS	AVG	LG	TD
1965	14	16	238	14.9	85	1	21	660	31.4*	96	1*
1966	14	6	44	7.3	27	0	23	718	31.2*	93	2*
1967	13	3	80	26.7	58	1*	16	603	37.7	103	3*
1968	9	2	29	14.5	18	0	17	461	27.1	46	0
1969	14	0	0	0	0	0	14	339	24.2	52	0
1970	2	0	0	0	0	0	0	0	0.0	0	0
1971	2	0	0	0	0	0	0	0	0.0	0	0
Totals	68	27	391	14.5	85	2	91	2781	30.6	103	6

* Led League

Boxscore of Gale Sayers' Six Touchdown Game at Wrigley Field, Chicago, December 12, 1965
Attendance: 46,278

San Francisco	0	13	0	7	—	20
Chicago	13	14	13	21	—	61

FIRST QUARTER	
Chi – Sayers 80 pass from Bukich (pass failed)	6–0
Chi – Ditka 29 pass from Bukich (Leclerc kick)	13–0

SECOND QUARTER	
SF – Parks 9 pass from Brodie (Davis kick)	13–7
Chi – Sayers 21 run (Leclerc kick)	20–7
SF – Crow 15 pass from Brodie (kick failed)	20–13
Chi – Sayers 7 run (Leclerc kick)	27–13

THIRD QUARTER	
Chi – Sayers 50 run (Leclerc kick)	34–13
Chi – Sayers 1 run (run failed)	40–13

FOURTH QUARTER	
SF – Kopay 2 run (Davis kick)	40–20
Chi – Jones 8 pass from Bukick (Leclerc kick)	47–20
Chi – Sayers 85 punt return (Leclerc kick)	54–20
Chi – Arnett 2 run (Leclerc kick)	61–20

Sources

Chapter 1

"I was sorry to see you get hurt, Mr. Sayers..." Silverman, Al, *I Am Third* (New York: Viking Press, 1970), p. 11.

Chapter 2

"Have you thought about what you want, Gale?..." Silverman, Al, *I Am Third* (New York: Viking Press, 1970), p. 35.

"Consider yourself lucky. If my father didn't like you..." Silverman, Al, *I Am Third* (New York: Viking Press, 1970), p. 35.

"Of all NFL coaches, only Shula and Halas attained 300 victories..." Pro Football Hall of Fame website, www.profootballhof.com, Don Shula biography, accessed December 2006.

Chapter 3

Brian's Song, movies.msn.com, accessed December 2006.

"One time a writer came in our room to interview us about being interracial roommates..." Silverman, Al, *I Am Third* (New York: Viking Press, 1970), p. 63.

Chapter 4

"The first College All-Star game was held in 1934 and it was the brainchild of sports editor Arch Ward of the *Chicago Tribune*..." Professional Football Researchers Association website, www.footballresearch.com, accessed November 2006.

"It was after that banquet that I decided to confront him. 'Is it true that you think I am dogging it, that I am not hurt?'..." Silverman, Al, *I Am Third* (New York: Viking Press, 1970), p. 183.

"The Browns won four straight American Association Football Conference titles and had a 52–4–3 record with him at quarterback..." Pro Football Hall of Fame website, www.profootballhof.com, Otto Graham biography, accessed December 2006.

"You got a shot at Rookie of the Year. But they're pushing Bob Hayes and Tucker Fredrickson..." Silverman, Al, *I Am Third* (New York: Viking Press, 1970), p. 192.

"'I hit him so hard, I thought my shoulder must have busted him in two,' said Grier..." www.bobzilla.tv, accessed December 2006.

"Nevers, who was a fullback, scored all 40 of the Cardinals' points in a 40–6 rout of the Bears that year..." Pro Football Hall of Fame website, www.profootballhof.com, Ernie Nevers biography, accessed December 2006.

Chapter 5

"The reason you got hurt was because you let your hair grow..." Silverman, Al, *I Am Third* (New York: Viking Press, 1970), p. 47.

"In 1966 our first-round draft pick was a guy named George Rice out of Louisiana State; in '67 it was Lloyd Phillips out of Arkansas..." Chicago Bears website, www.chicagobears.com, accessed November 2006.

"Wade had been a first-round draft pick of the Los Angeles Rams in 1952 out of Vanderbilt..." www.profootballreference.com, accessed November 2006.

Chapter 6

"Campbell took tremendous physical pounding throughout his career, yet missed only six games out of 115 because of injuries..." www.profootballreference.com, accessed November 2006.

"Sanders ran low to the ground and rushed for more than 1,000 yards in each of his 10 seasons with the Lions (1989–1998)..." www.profootballreference.com, accessed November 2006.

"In 1985, Payton rushed for 1,551 yards, caught 49 passes, and scored 11 touchdowns..." Chicago Bears website, www.chicagobears.com, accessed October 2006.

"The Bears led the league in rushing in 1977 behind the running of Payton, and then did not lead the league in that category again until 1983..." Chicago Bears website, www.chicagobears.com, accessed October 2006.

"Astonishingly, Holmes joined the Baltimore Ravens as an undrafted free agent in 1997..." www.profootball reference.com, accessed November 2006.

"'I told my mother then that I wanted to be a football player,' said Tomlinson..." "Around Town," *Chicago Tribune*, sports section, February 1, 2007, p. 2.

Chapter 7

"The Dale Carnegie Course is a self-improvement pro-gram conducted using a standardized curriculum by professional trainers throughout the world..." Dale Carnegie Training website, www.dalecarnegie.com, accessed October 2006.

"In 2004, for instance, the NFL agreed to $8 billion in contract extensions with Fox and CBS..." *Chicago Tribune*, sports section, November 8, 2004, p. 1.

"Commissioner Rozelle, ladies and gentlemen. I am deeply honored to be inducted..." Pro Football Hall of Fame website, www.profootballhof.com, Gale Sayers biography, accessed October 2006.

Chapter 8

"I ran to the sideline so excited and I asked Break, 'Did you see me use the Run-Around? Did you see me?'..." Silverman, Al, *I Am Third* (New York: Viking Press, 1970), p. 47.

Chapter 12

"Halas said: 'Gale, you know what? They could arrest you for murder'..." Silverman, Al, *I Am Third* (New York: Viking Press, 1970).

Index

Index